Jean- lump in breast - exploratory appt
on Monday

Jane - pray for Park family

Trish- her dad is sick

# Desperate Women of the Bible

## LESSONS ON PASSION FROM THE GOSPELS

### JO KADLECEK

BakerBooks
Grand Rapids, Michigan

Published by Baker Books
a division of Baker Publishing Group
P.O. Box 6287, Grand Rapids, MI 49516-6287
www.bakerbooks.com

Printed in the United States of America

Library of Congress Cataloging-in-Publication Data is on file at the Library of Congress, Washington, D.C.

ISBN 10: 0-8010-6618-2 (pbk.)
ISBN 978-0-8010-6618-4 (pbk.)

For those friends, here and abroad,
who have struggled, ached, or run out of resources.

# CONTENTS

"Behind our own history,
deepening it at every point,
has been another history."

Flannery O'Connor

# PROLOGUE

DESPERATE . . . FOR A STORY

There is no agony like bearing an untold story inside you.

Zora Neale Hurston

Last July, my brother's family visited my husband and me as part of their summer vacation. One night while we were sitting around the barbeque after dinner, Annie, my six-year-old niece, looked up at me, blue eyes wide and excited, and said, "Let's play the story game, Aunt Jo! Can we? Please?!"

How could I say no?

For the next ten minutes (as everyone else cleared the table), Annie gave me details about the character she'd literally just created. Then she stopped midsentence, waved at me like she was an emcee introducing the upcoming act on a stage, and waited for me to fill in the next part of the tale. I obliged with silly adventures and strange sounds while she laughed and waited for her turn to continue the nonsensical story before waving me in again. The story ended when the ice cream was served, but not before I realized—once

11

again—that a child's imagination is a gift. Annie cannot help but crave stories. She's made that way.

Children of all cultures, times, and ages—from six to ninety-six years old—have always longed for the wonder, delight, and adventure of a good story. We identify with a character, feel a sense of connection to a setting, or cheer for a heroine as she overcomes a dozen obstacles on her journey. We watch relationships grow, listen to voices we otherwise might not hear, and feel the crazy emotions that scale the range of human experiences. Stories help us make sense of this thing called living and encourage us to face the challenges and glories of another day. Stories help us breathe.

Whether in a child's game or around a watercooler, on a cinematic screen, a stage, in a newspaper or the pages of a book, stories remind us that we're not alone. Like people, they come in all sizes, genres, and styles, reflecting one basic truth about the human condition: we cannot live without them. At least, we cannot live well without stories.

Little wonder, then, that the book considered by many of history's most intelligent and creative people to be one of the most influential pieces of literature is also a true story. From national dignitaries and medical geniuses, renowned composers and literary artists, to activists and labor workers, engineers and teachers, millions of women and men across the continents and ages have staked their lives, their vocations, and their relationships on the single message and story of the Bible. Christians call it God's Word.

And his name is Jesus.

John, the author of one of the four Gospels in the New Testament, wrote in the first chapter of his book, "The Word became flesh and made his dwelling among us. We have seen his glory, the glory of the One and Only, who came from the Father, full of grace and truth" (1:14). And so, the Story of God became the story of humankind, living, breathing, and laughing among other humans all for the single purpose that we might be a part of his story, that we might know what it means to belong.

I have to admit, I love this story as much as my niece loves the story game. Truth be told, I have come to see it—as I think many others have—as a story of enormous literary power and radical personal impact, one that has affected me more than all the others I've ever read or heard combined. It has changed wicked minds and repaired aching hearts—like mine. It has continued to infuse hope in otherwise desperate situations, renew dreams in otherwise lifeless routines, and provide meaning in otherwise chaotic moments. Yes, I admit it: I love the Bible. Though I don't always understand it, I love the entirety of the story from Genesis to Revelation. I love that though it remains the most widely read book of all time, it never loses its relevance, eloquence, or sway.

Perhaps that is because it is, like all great literature, a simple but unifying tale with characters we can relate to, conflicts we have confronted ourselves, and page-turning plot twists by which we can't help but be surprised. But unlike other literary works, its goal is to engage readers directly with its Author. In other words, the biblical story is a wonder-filled invitation to know our Creator.

And it goes something like this: the protagonist leaves his position of power in a distant kingdom to enter the dusty place known as Earth and live among an equally dusty people. He has one solitary goal: to win back these dusty souls for the love of his Father back home—who has been working, I might add, for some time to get their attention and prepare them for his Son's arrival.

But to do that, the protagonist must face the danger of evil men, the perils of fickle followers, and the temptations of fleshly yearnings. He must fight an enemy whose strategy is deception and confront an opponent who revels in brokenness. And it will appear at first that he cannot win. His purpose, though, is unstoppable, and so even as the stakes are raised, he faces each battle with perhaps the most bizarre suit of armor and ammunition any hero could use: words, love, stories, and of course, sacrifice. Though it is not easy, he is able to endure every barrier thrown into his path, and in the process creates a legend that still offers a gift of eternal proportions.

Along the way, however, this hero will challenge, heal, cry, eat, pray, preach, listen, befriend, and die. He will offer his back to be sliced with whips, his head to be pierced by thorns, and his heart to be shattered by absolute loneliness. It will not seem very heroic. But each step on his journey will always be for the ultimate object of his affection, the unwavering motivation behind his action: human beings. Women. Children. Men.

You. Me.


## Stories Within

The story of Jesus Christ is, as contemporary writer Frederick Buechner calls it, a tragedy, a comedy, and a fairy tale.[1] It is tragic because it is an honest sorrow and suffering, both of which must be faced before anything else becomes possible. But from such tragedy emerges the comedy of a new life: a prostitute becomes a preacher, for instance, or a widow becomes a mother again. Darkness is overcome by light, or a bland, ordinary routine is turned upside down by the extraordinary. This is when the gospel story becomes like the fairy tales we read as children, for as Buechner says, it is "a tale that is too good not to be true because to dismiss it as untrue is to dismiss along with it that 'catch of the breath, that beat and lifting of the heart near to or even accompanied by tears,' which I believe is the deepest intuition of truth that we have."[2]

And what a story to empower and inspire us for the days in which we now live! Ours is a culture in which most people I know long for their hearts to be lifted by a story so good and so true it nearly takes away their breath. Maybe that's because we cannot go a day without flipping through the newspaper and witnessing again the tragedy of human nature gone awry.

Or, if the news of real-world horrors (or our own lives) isn't enough to push us to despair, we can switch on the television shows and escape reality with desperate housewives, purposeless people, or serial killers. As a result, I think we're all the more hungry, desperate even ourselves, for good news, for the one true story that continues to surprise us with its compassion toward the brokenhearted, gladden us with its healing touch, and astound us with the promise of a life transformed.

Which brings us back to the Bible. In the four Gospel narratives, we meet a cast of quirky and crude characters around whom the life and ministry of Jesus Christ revolves. Specifically, we're introduced to an array of marginalized creatures, several of whom are women. Their stories, their lives, are surely the stuff of tragedy, that is, until they encounter Someone who turns everything upside down, who gives them a reason to believe.

Many of these women are passionate but needy humans who want to live well but whose excruciatingly difficult circumstances have left them distressed, and in some cases hopeless. They're at that point in their lives—I think we've all been there—when they'll try just about anything and believe just about anyone who is willing to help them. They are vulnerable, afraid, and out of resources. They've reached their limit and have resigned themselves to the idea that this is "just how it's going to be." Get used to it. It probably will not get better. Ever.

Enter the fairy tale, and something beyond magical happens. Each woman in these Gospel accounts is uniquely affected. Affirmed. Loved. Accepted. The funny thing is we don't even know their names. But because of God's tenderness toward them, we do know their stories. Yet, lest we slip into viewing them merely as characters from some old book, we must remember theirs are true stories, actual lives, historic testimonies that were documented in the pages of Holy Scripture.

For our sake.

So, in the chapters that follow here, you and I will meet these nameless women from the Gospels as they interact with a Man unlike any they've ever known. (And some of these women have known men!) Certainly, we can learn much from them about the various levels of passion; that is, what it means to live with intense desires, maneuver overwhelming obstacles, cling to a dream, or let go of a lifetime of alienation, suffering, and shame. Passion gone awry. Though they lived on the margins of their culture, we will find they were, nonetheless, courageous women, albeit desperately in need. Yes, their stories are immensely instructive for us today. (At the end of each chapter are questions that are meant to guide you in your reflections on these gospel stories.)

## Pointing to Another Story

But as we explore their details, we must not forget that these women were secondary characters in the shadow of the primary character; subplots, if you will, in the bigger story of the Bible. In the same way minor characters in a novel might shed light on the protagonist, so too do these nameless women teach us about the hero of the Gospels, Jesus Christ. For in each of their stories, the Man from Galilee looked square into the face of despair, took a misguided or "diseased" passion, and turned it into a life with purpose, grace, and dignity. Redeemed and restored for his purposes.

That is the Good News we are looking for. Especially in these days when passion is so easily misunderstood or grows into frightening fanaticism, I believe we need to return to that place, to the book where we discover how our intense desires really can be nurtured and used as they were meant to. Its enduring story and truth is both an anchor for us in a world that daily tempts us to wander, and a guide to living the abundant life we've been invited to by—and with—our Creator.

In part, this book grew out of my own study of the Scriptures and my own desperation to learn what it means to live passionately with Jesus as a part of his bigger story. As I've read about these women in the Gospels, taught on them at retreats, and talked about them with friends, I've also been reminded how much I have always been attracted to people with authentic passion—and genuinely frightened at the times I have felt numb or bored with life. Maybe the lives of these nameless women inspire me to pick up the pace and get going again. Maybe they speak to me across the centuries of a faith without which I'd still be living a tragedy. Whatever it is that has drawn me to them, they confirm for me that the person and life of Jesus Christ is the best news I have ever heard in my life and the truest story I have ever encountered.

Or rather, that has ever encountered me.

Why do I think so? Because when I read the stories that will follow here—the story, for instance, of the Samaritan woman at the well—I watch a woman of thirst become a woman of deep satisfaction. When I read about the woman with the issue of blood, I see her transformed into a woman of new strength. I see a woman of tears become a woman of comfort and new freedom. And women of grief, of death, and of darkness become women of hope, of life, and of light.

How does such change happen? As it always does in a good story. Because a Prince pursues his love, sacrifices for her, and gives her more than she deserves or ever imagines she will receive. He steps into her world to hang on a cross and cry "I thirst!" He takes in his body her pain, weeps over her losses, and dies the death she—and all of us—should have died. Then, he conquers death and writes his story of resurrection over and over again in countless faces, ways, and stories. Why? To win back the dusty souls of humans like us with—and for—the love of his Father back home.

These nameless women remind us how that same Truth can shape the stories of our lives today. That is, if we are just desperate enough.

# In-Between Reflection

1. Stories shape our thinking and teach us about living. What books or stories in particular had a great impact on you as a child? Why? *Little House Books - I loved the idea of living in a different time*

2. What makes a good story? *Makes you care about the characters to know them*

3. What recent story have you read that led you to a deeper place of self-awareness?

4. What recent story have you read that led you to a deeper understanding of God?

5. How does the true story of Jesus Christ affect you at this point in your life?

# Digging Deeper

All people from all cultures and times have told stories. God designed us this way and the Bible confirms it both in medium and message. From Genesis to Revelation, the story of God and his people reflects several recurring themes. List a few of these themes (i.e., God pursues, his people sin and get in trouble, he provides a way out, etc.).


What specific biblical stories point you to the Gospel story of Christ as our ultimate Rescuer, Redeemer, and Lord (Abraham and Isaac, Ruth and Naomi, Jonah, etc.)? Go back and read them anew to see what new insights you discover.

# Preparation

*Please take a few moments right now to read from the Gospel of John, chapter 4, verses 1–42, printed below. It is the story of the Samaritan woman who meets Jesus at the town well in the middle of the day. Once you've read it, pause for a quiet moment to consider the words you've read.*

### Jesus Talks with a Samaritan Woman

¹The Pharisees heard that Jesus was gaining and baptizing more disciples than John, ²although in fact it was not Jesus who baptized, but his disciples. ³When the Lord learned of this, he left Judea and went back once more to Galilee.

⁴Now he had to go through Samaria. ⁵So he came to a town in Samaria called Sychar, near the plot of ground Jacob had given to his son Joseph. ⁶Jacob's well was there, and Jesus, tired as he was from the journey, sat down by the well. It was about the sixth hour.

⁷When a Samaritan woman came to draw water, Jesus said to her, "Will you give me a drink?" ⁸(His disciples had gone into the town to buy food.)

⁹The Samaritan woman said to him, "You are a Jew and I am a Samaritan woman. How can you ask me for a drink?" (For Jews do not associate with Samaritans.)

¹⁰Jesus answered her, "If you knew the gift of God and who it is that asks you for a drink, you would have asked him and he would have given you living water."

¹¹"Sir," the woman said, "you have nothing to draw with and the well is deep. Where can you get this living water? ¹²Are you greater than our father Jacob, who gave us the well and drank from it himself, as did also his sons and his flocks and herds?"

¹³Jesus answered, "Everyone who drinks this water will be thirsty again, ¹⁴but whoever drinks the water I give him will never thirst. Indeed, the water I give him will become in him a spring of water welling up to eternal life."

¹⁵The woman said to him, "Sir, give me this water so that I won't get thirsty and have to keep coming here to draw water."

¹⁶He told her, "Go, call your husband and come back."

¹⁷"I have no husband," she replied.

Jesus said to her, "You are right when you say you have no husband. ¹⁸The fact is, you have had five husbands, and the man you now have is not your husband. What you have just said is quite true."

¹⁹"Sir," the woman said, "I can see that you are a prophet. ²⁰Our fathers worshiped on this mountain, but you Jews claim that the place where we must worship is in Jerusalem."

²¹Jesus declared, "Believe me, woman, a time is coming when you will worship the Father neither on this mountain nor in Jerusalem. ²²You Samaritans worship what you do not know; we worship what we do know, for salvation is from the Jews. ²³Yet a time is coming and has now come when the true worshipers will worship the Father in spirit and truth, for they are the kind of worshipers the Father seeks. ²⁴God is spirit, and his worshipers must worship in spirit and in truth."

²⁵The woman said, "I know that Messiah" (called Christ) "is coming. When he comes, he will explain everything to us."

²⁶Then Jesus declared, "I who speak to you am he."

### The Disciples Rejoin Jesus

²⁷Just then his disciples returned and were surprised to find him talking with a woman. But no one asked, "What do you want?" or "Why are you talking with her?"

$^{28}$Then, leaving her water jar, the woman went back to the town and said to the people, $^{29}$"Come, see a man who told me everything I ever did. Could this be the Christ?" $^{30}$They came out of the town and made their way toward him.

$^{31}$Meanwhile his disciples urged him, "Rabbi, eat something."

$^{32}$But he said to them, "I have food to eat that you know nothing about."

$^{33}$Then his disciples said to each other, "Could someone have brought him food?"

$^{34}$"My food," said Jesus, "is to do the will of him who sent me and to finish his work. $^{35}$Do you not say, 'Four months more and then the harvest'? I tell you, open your eyes and look at the fields! They are ripe for harvest. $^{36}$Even now the reaper draws his wages, even now he harvests the crop for eternal life, so that the sower and the reaper may be glad together. $^{37}$Thus the saying 'One sows and another reaps' is true. $^{38}$I sent you to reap what you have not worked for. Others have done the hard work, and you have reaped the benefits of their labor."

### Many Samaritans Believe

$^{39}$Many of the Samaritans from that town believed in him because of the woman's testimony, "He told me everything I ever did." $^{40}$So when the Samaritans came to him, they urged him to stay with them, and he stayed two days. $^{41}$And because of his words many more became believers.

$^{42}$They said to the woman, "We no longer believe just because of what you said; now we have heard for ourselves, and we know that this man really is the Savior of the world."

When you are ready, continue reflecting on the following question:

Perhaps you've read this story before. What new insights or observations jumped out to you as you read her story anew in this Gospel account? Jot them down. Take a few moments to reflect before reading chapter 1.

**Prayer:** *Thank you, Jesus, that if we drink of you, you will give us a spring of water welling up to eternal life! Amen.*

---
1
---

# THIRSTY FOR MORE
# THAN A DRINK

Why does he batter at walls that won't break? Why does
he give when it's natural to take? Where does he see all the
good he can see, and what does he want of me?
   What does he want of me?

Aldonza, *Man of La Mancha*

Sometimes, I wish books could sing. If they could, I'd start
here with one of the most beautiful pieces I've ever heard in
musical theater. It is "Dulcinea," sung by the Don Quixote
character in *Man of La Mancha*, a tender but profound love
song plopped into the middle of a drama not unlike our
story of the Man sent to earth by his Father back home. To
listen to it float from the voice of a rich baritone accompanied by an orchestra is chilling—in a really good way. The
sound can be as stirring and dramatic as the colors in the sky
when the sun has set. Or as intense and profound as staring
at Michelangelo's statue of David, and unless you are dead
in your bones, you cannot help but be moved by it.

It is, after all, a song of grace.

My husband and I had the privilege of watching the Broadway revival of *Man of La Mancha* a few years back. We were celebrating our anniversary, and because my husband had never seen this particular show, I wanted him to experience the story and the music I'd come to love each time I'd seen it either at a regional or college production. It is the story of Miguel de Cervantes, the sixteenth-century Spanish writer arrested by the Inquisition and thrown into prison. The holding cell is full of thieves and cutthroats, and he and his servant must go on trial for their lives by the other prisoners. For his defense, Cervantes offers the inmates a story he then proceeds to act out—the story of Don Quixote de la Mancha.

Don Quixote is determined to bring goodwill and chivalry back to the "bleak and unbearable world"; as a knight, he hurls down his gauntlet and takes up his destiny, going wherever the "wild winds of fortune" will take him. His is a "holy endeavor" and he dreams an "impossible dream" that proclaims even his willingness "to march into hell for a heavenly cause." Don Quixote is a man on a mission.

But to those who don't know him, he is a fool who chases windmills. Even to Dulcinea, the beautiful woman whom the knight has chosen as his lady. The only problem is she is known to most men as something else, something entirely different from what the Man of La Mancha knows her as. To them she is the hard and bitter tavern whore known as Aldonza, but to Don Quixote she is Dulcinea, which means "sweet one."

From the minute he encounters her, Don Quixote identifies her only as Dulcinea, his lady. She thinks he is insane, of course, and argues with him while the other men in the tavern laugh at him. They know better. They know her in ways he never has—and never will.

Still, he is utterly blind to their responses, and he does what every protagonist in a musical does because he cannot help himself, because he must: he sings. He stares into the eyes of his love as if no one else is in the tavern (or the theater), and he sings an astonishingly beautiful tune (written by Mitch Leigh) with equally beautiful lyrics (written by Joe Darion):

> I have dreamed thee too long, never seen thee or touched thee, but known thee with all my heart,
> Half a prayer, half a song, thou hast always been with me, though we have been always apart.
>
> Dulcinea . . . Dulcinea . . . I see heaven when I see thee, Dulcinea, and thy name is like a prayer an angel whispers . . . Dulcinea . . . Dulcinea!
>
> If I reach out to thee, do not tremble and shrink from the touch of my hand on thy hair.
> Let my fingers but see thou art warm and alive, and no phantom to fade in the air.
>
> Dulcinea . . . Dulcinea . . . I have sought thee, sung thee, dreamed thee, Dulcinea! Now I've found thee, and the world shall know thy glory. Dulcinea . . . Dulcinea![1]

The song ends with the mocking chants of "Dulcinea" from the drunken men, but not without the Man of La Mancha's proclamation completely drowning them out and baffling his lady with his grace in the process. Nonetheless, she does not—will not—believe him. In fact, the next time they meet, Aldonza does her best to convince him of who she really is: "the most casual bride of the murdering scum of the earth . . . I am no one! I'm nothing! I'm only Aldonza the whore!"

Then in a fit of absolute self-protection, she calls him the "cruelest of all" men because his kindness is too much to endure: "Blows and abuse I can take and give back again, tenderness I cannot bear!" Yet, Don Quixote vows to defend her honor. No matter what she says, he bows before her and softly says over and over, "Thou art still my lady . . . now and forever thou art my lady Dulcinea!" When she cannot take his terrible benevolence anymore, she screams in despair at him and drives him away.

It isn't until the final scene of the drama, when the hero is dying center stage, that we hear the most marvelous line in the entire story. It comes from—who else?—Aldonza, who despite her past and her protests has watched what the Man of La Mancha has done, seen the power of his hope, and comes to a place where she whispers, "My name . . . is Dulcinea."

It is a moment of conversion. Of grace apprehended. Of love realized. Of mercy breaking into her world, a world where she learns that everything she thought was real was anything but. Until now. Now she was a lady. Now she was who she was supposed to be. Now she was Dulcinea, the sweet one.

My husband and I sat for many quiet moments after the curtain came down and the applause of the audience died. We sighed at the goodness of the story and eventually wandered from the theater deeply affected by the performance we'd just witnessed. Like all great art has a habit of doing, the musical reminded us again of the bigger story behind the intoxicating exchange between Cervantes's Don Quixote and Dulcinea. For we both knew that her encounter with love was one that is happening today everywhere we look: whether on the streets of Europe, in churches in Australia, revivals across Africa, or gatherings throughout North America, you name it, God is captivating his people with a mercy like few have ever seen before.

Those who don't know him, of course, call it foolishness.

But the reality of the Scriptures has always claimed that some would be captivated by Christ while others would call him a fool. For throughout the biblical narrative, One sings the names of those he loves and in doing so, he "seeks them and dreams them,"[2] transforming their lives with the absolute certainty of his affection. And they—and we—are shaped for eternity by the proclamation of this extravagant love that comes in spite of the people who receive it. Whether Abraham or David, Mary or Peter, the diverse and real women and men whose stories are woven into the Bible's narrative have this one thing in common: God has pursued them in love. Don Quixote is smitten by his lady.

And from my experiences talking with women here and abroad, I think there are many "Dulcineas" living in our contemporary times. They were first "Aldonzas" who fought with God over the stories of their lives until finally he won them over with his sacrificial love, giving them a new identity in the process. Sure, some are still fighting—we all do. We are, after all, human; we get defensive and protective because we do not want to get hurt. And too often in our heart of hearts, we do not really believe we could be loved, let alone be lovable. Besides, we know that though the truth of the gospel is like a fairy tale as well, we sometimes believe it is simply too good to be true.

But it is true. And many other stories of women who encounter the Lord of the Gospels confirm it. Like Aldonza, they too were desperate women whose lives were marked by lies and pain and deception. They accepted each as inevitable but always hoped for more, thirsted for something else to satisfy them. Something especially that would bring them to a place of honor and dignity, rather than the shame or degradation they had known all their lives.

## A Woman of Thirst

Perhaps there is no greater example of this transforming power than in the true story of the Samaritan woman at the well recorded in the fourth chapter of John's Gospel. Her seemingly chance encounter with Jesus changed every-thing she'd ever known. It is a story of even greater passion and grace than Dulcinea's because it comes to us not from Broadway but directly from the book we call God's Word. God ordained the story first by "creating" it and then by insuring its inclusion in the Gospel written by the "disciple whom Jesus loved." Consequently, it is significant, and though historic, it is one that speaks to us today as we go about the business of our daily lives.

Before we dive into her story, though, I think it is impor-tant first to consider four questions that can help us better understand these Scripture stories and passages. These questions often guide my personal Bible study as well as my preparation whenever I've been invited to teach at re-treats or conferences; like a richly textured four-course meal, they help us better appreciate the fullness of the biblical "flavors" and the impact each could have.

The first question to ask is what is the *context* of the passage? What's happened before in the culture and to the characters in the story that might affect its meaning and its message? What's the bigger picture that this scene is set in? That question helps us better understand all of Scripture as a unified book and keeps us from creating theologies (or belief systems) that might spring up from one single verse. It's always dangerous to compartmentalize verses—or take them out of context—and forget that God's Word is one sacred text, comprised of many layers that blend together to reflect God's purposes.

The second question is one that lingers from my days as an English teacher. (Blame it on the English teachers!) When coming to specific verses, we need to consider what the *conflict* in the passage is. What or who is at odds? What or who is being confronted? Buechner astutely reminds us that before the gospel can be good news, it must be bad news first. That is the essence of conflict—two or more forces at odds that become the why behind the story and the driving force of all literature. In other words, there is inherently some aspect of a fallen world that needs to be redeemed, some bad that needs a touch of good, some evil chaos that needs taming and ordering by righteousness. Some lostness that needs saving.

Adventure films help us understand this; we watch not to find out what ultimately happens—because we already believe good will conquer evil. No, we watch to see the hero figure out how to get out of each pickle she finds herself in. Most times, the stakes keep getting raised in these films, making each obstacle harder, higher, or more harmful than the last. But that is the real reason we keep watching—to see how in the world she will ever overcome each particular problem thrown at her by her opponents, even though we already know she will. It's the thrill of the adventure!

Once we know the context and the conflict, we then ask what the *counsel* is we could draw from the passage. What new insights could we learn? What does Dulcinea, or rather the Samaritan woman at the well, teach us? Each life, each story, each passage has a purpose. Our job is, with God's help, to discover its wisdom and glean from its truth at the moment we encounter it.

But lest it become merely an academic experience in which we identify the answers to these three "C" questions, we must ask the most important question of all, the question that arises from the same place of desperation we see in Aldonza as well as in each of these nameless women in the Gospels. How can this story lead us to *conversion*, or how can it help us change? No matter how much she fights or pretends it is not so, Aldonza really does want to become Dulcinea. Just as our Samaritan woman ultimately desires the type of satisfaction that will quench more than her daily thirst for water. These women want change, are desperate for it. And I'm guessing most of us are too.

And so the stories of these nameless women in the Gospels inspire us with their personal transformations while at the same time pointing us toward the road of conversion. That is after all what really matters, right? To grow, to examine our lives in the light of God's Word so that we become more like the people he's created us to be, the women and men whose lives—and names—are changed by a song of absolute acceptance.

First, though, we must recognize our need. The story of this real woman whose name we don't even know but whose moment in history has been documented by the apostle John is our teacher for now. It is the story of a thirsty Samaritan woman, who "happened" upon a hero who changed her life. And then changed the lives of almost everyone who knew her.

## The Context

John probably wrote his Gospel toward the end of the first century after the mission trips of Paul and before he wrote the last book of the Bible, Revelation. Like all of the Gospels, his conveys unique qualities of its author. We see John's knowledge as an intimate eyewitness of Christ's three years of ministry; his understanding of Jewish thinking, customs, and geography; and his appreciation of Greek culture, which was the dominant culture in terms of the rest of the world. Greeks were the cultural elites of their day, sensual, philosophical, authoritative. People spoke Greek then in the way English is spoken today. John knew this and wrote accordingly.

What else distinguishes John's Gospel from Matthew's, Mark's, or Luke's? Because its primary purpose is evangelistic, it reveals more of the relational, personal side of Jesus. The story of our Samaritan woman certainly confirms both. In fact, theirs is one of the longer dialogues included in the

Gospels between Jesus and a person, let alone a woman, reflecting both his desire to win her over and his personal concern for her.

This "chance" meeting took place in the first year of Jesus's ministry, when he left Judea and the region around Jerusalem to go back again to his native Galilee in the north of Israel. Between Judea and Galilee lies Samaria, a region of about 1600 square miles, stretching between the Jordan River on the east and the Mediterranean Sea on the west. The Samaritans were descendants of Jews, but they intermarried with the Assyrians who occupied the area from 726 to 721 BC, during one of the many times Israel was conquered. Their intermarriages with the Gentiles enabled them to survive, and they often fared better than the Jews who resisted such. Consequently, a great animosity grew between the Samaritans and the Jews, who considered the Samaritans half-breeds and heretics.

Because they believed Samaritans had long been religiously and ethnically mixed, or syncretistic, and blended pagan worship with Jewish tradition, Jews did not venture into Samaria. To devout Jews, Samaritans were a compromised, unclean people they avoided, not engaged with. They had "affairs" with many gods, and therefore were considered religiously "promiscuous." The perception was so intense that when Jews had to travel back and forth between Judea in the south and Galilee in the north they avoided Samaria altogether! Instead of taking the direct route through Samaria, they would go down to Jericho, cross the Jordan River into Perea (which is now the kingdom of Jordan), and then head north, not crossing back over the river until they were well north of Samaria and due east of Nazareth. This turned what would otherwise have been about a sixty-mile trip into almost a hundred miles—which was no small thing before the days of cars, buses, or trains. But they believed it was worth walking the extra miles so as not to risk encountering the Samaritans.

Not Jesus, though. Because of who he was, he could not, as one minister put it, "follow a trail that fear and hatred had blazed." So Jesus intentionally went through Samaria, that part of town we'd know today as an "inner city." Instead of going around the 'hood from one stretch of town to the suburbs, Jesus took the most direct route: right through the area where graffiti, broken glass, and boarded buildings were as common as manicured lawns in a suburb. It was a place where a typical righteous man would never go. Ever.

Yet John says that, "He had to go to Samaria." Well, no, he did not have to go through Samaria, at least geographically. Then why did John include this strange detail? Perhaps he knew that Jesus's decision to take this road had more to do with his greater mission than with his travel sensibilities or his attention to religious customs.

By doing so, he met a woman at the well who was a mirror of her culture. Life had left her hard and tough, an Aldonza of the Samaritans. In that time period, she had three strikes against her: she was a woman, a Samaritan, and promiscuous. Her difficult lifestyle was likely why she came to the well at a time of day when most respectable women would not usually have drawn their water. Most would have drawn it either early in the morning or at the end of the day.

So why is their conversation so significant? First, it is important to know that women rarely interacted with religious men publicly, let alone a woman like her interacting with a man like Jesus. She knew it, others knew it, and Jesus certainly knew it. As the great British minister Charles Spurgeon put it in a sermon he preached (rather prophetically, I think) in 1886:

First, it was sufficiently offensive that the person with whom Jesus was conversing was a woman. My beloved sisters, you owe much to the Gospel, for it is only by its agency that you are raised to your proper place. For what said the rabbis? "Rather burn the sayings of the law than teach them to a woman." Again, "Let no man prolong conversation with a woman; let no one converse with a woman in the streets, nor even with his own wife." Women were thought to be unfit for profound religious instruction and altogether inferior beings. My sisters, we do not think that you are superior to us, though some of you perhaps fancy so. But we are right glad to own your equality and to know that in Christ Jesus there is neither male nor female. Jesus has lifted you up to your true place, side by side with man. Even the apostles were tainted at first with that horrible superstition that made them marvel that Jesus openly talked with a woman.[3]

So we know what's happening in a cultural context: women were considered second-class, inferior beings, utterly unfit for religious instruction by respectable rabbis. Samaritans were marginalized and hated by the cultural leaders of the time, and women like this one who had multiple "husbands" were deemed no better than property.

But what of the woman's personal context? She obviously was at the well because she was thirsty, yet her track record suggests she was thirsty for more than just water. She'd been married many times over, and so she knew she was considered damaged goods, unclean, and unworthy. She was a lot like Samaria (and a lot like Aldonza): desperate, loose, confused, lonely, and hurt.

Still, I can't help but think she was immensely thirsty for life, passionate for intimacy and meaning. Why else would she have had so many husbands? We don't know the circumstances of each marriage, but we can surmise that she was never fully satisfied with her relationships. Why? Because no man could ever fill her parched and empty soul; they were never meant to. Only God would satisfy the longings of this woman as he does for every human.

This, then, is the longing behind every other longing or desire we have—the longing for Jesus.

Her personal story taps into what I've experienced personally and observed corporately as a fundamental insecurity in women: the disbelief that she—that we—could be chosen. Even the way she responded to Jesus's questions with all of her "yes, buts . . ." suggests she was astonished that Jesus talked with her at all and made the requests he did of her. When his apostles returned, they reinforced her insecurity because they couldn't believe their leader would be talking with her either. "Tainted by the horrible superstition," as Spurgeon called it.

Throughout their conversation, the Samaritan woman used a variety of desperate comments to deflect from the deeper matters Christ wanted to confront: "You have nothing to draw with," "I have no husband," "Our fathers worshiped on this mountain." And when she couldn't think of any better questions, after all of her arguments, she gave in and became practical: "Sir, give me this water so that I won't get thirsty and have to keep coming here to draw water" (v. 15).

Perhaps her boldness signaled to Jesus that she was willing to consider what he had to say. So he pushed and confronted her on her relationships with men. By this point, she didn't deny it or get defensive. Still, she must have stared at her Don Quixote with skeptical eyes because though the reality of the experience suggested she was in fact hearing this man invite her to drink of his eternal water, she was trapped by her cultural mores and a lifetime of lies that this could be happening at all. It is as if she was saying, "Well, gee, Mister, what you say sure sounds good, but it just ain't possible, at least until the Messiah comes, and when he does, he'll explain everything . . ."

Her personal story, her context—like all of ours—set the stage to the obvious conflict she encountered with Jesus, a conflict where he would challenge her presuppositions, her insecurities, and the things (idols) she might have put her faith in—the material world, relationships, traditions, expectations. In the same way, we bring all of our lives—our history, our baggage, our past, our future—into our relationship with Christ when he pursues us and initiates a conversation with us. And this is what remains a remarkable aspect of the story: given the context of this woman and the culture in which she lived, even knowing all of who this woman was, Jesus still "had to go to Samaria." He, too, was thirsty from his journey yet decided it was as good an opportunity as any to sit down and chat with this woman. To pursue his Dulcinea. To sing her into being.

It was a scene rife with conflict.

## The Conflict

So we have a Perfect Man, God incarnate, pursuing a very imperfect woman for all the world to see. In spite of the cultural context that suggested religious men should not talk with such women, Jesus singled her out. He pursued this woman with a past though she hadn't done a single thing to earn his attention. She was merely performing her daily menial task of getting water! The last thing she probably thought would happen that day was that she'd run into some radical young rabbi on his way north. If she had known, she'd have at least cleaned herself up a bit, or perhaps she wouldn't have gotten out of bed at all. But she did get out of bed, thirsty, worn out, and a mess, on her way to the well, where she didn't expect to see another living soul. Let alone a man who would challenge her like he did.

Jesus, too, could have been anywhere else: with the crowds teaching; with his disciples picking out food for lunch; napping in a local hotel. Instead, he went after the "unworthy one," the individual who never saw him coming but had always hoped someone like him existed somewhere. In so doing, he struck a chord that resonates with every contemporary woman I've ever known: feeling unworthy but hoping against hope that the answer to our hearts' longing would come after us, would pursue us.

He did, and he still does.

The problem with this part of the story, though, is that holiness and sin don't mix, then or now, which means their confrontation would lead—like it always does—to other confrontations. We had a mess of a woman meeting a Messiah of a Man, and as his light began to shine on her, one small dark thing after another became exposed, until she began to understand just how dark and how small she really was. Just how much she needed a savior.

The bad news came before the good news; in fact, the bad news in this case became the good news. Before that could happen, though, Jesus had to confront her on an equally human level, asking for water since they were both thirsty. To her, however, his question was loaded, given the context in which it was asked. She countered with two sincere questions: "Are you sure you know who you're asking? (You talking to *me*?)," followed by, "Where can you get this living water?" By this point in her desperate life, she was open to anyone who would give her a clue to find any meaning at all in the ragged life she'd lived so far.

Then Christ confronted her lust, or her passion for intimacy, approval, and connection. How did she respond? Unlike Aldonza, she never argued with him or got defensive. In fact, the more he talked, the bolder she seemed to get in her responses to him, as if she thought to herself, *This guy's safe*. And when she finally confessed with ultimate honesty—"I have no husband"—Jesus gave her another clue of who he was when he revealed her shady life with men. Then in a strange turn in the conversation, he began to talk with her about worship.

Why? Because he knew that was what she was born for, ultimately, to direct her passionate devotion to her Creator so that she no longer worshiped men or sex or traditions or any other god that might keep her from her true purpose: to worship God. For she (like all of us) was wired for that one beautiful and eternal reason: worship.

If we do not worship God, we can be sure we will worship something, or someone, else. Knowing this, Jesus invited this woman to worship him, and consequently she was taken from her usual course of daily living and moved to do a special new work for God the Father.

Hence, the Good News. The Comedy of the Gospel!

What a joy to read how such an encounter with Jesus, the living water, overflowed into every aspect of this woman's life. She had come to the well that noonday to get water, to do one job, and something entirely different happened. Suddenly, the mundane turned into an adventure because of Jesus. So much so that when she realized just who it was she'd met, she left with such urgency and such enthusiasm that she seemed to forget why she'd come to the well at all. John tells us that she left her water jar behind. But because of who she was, I doubt she could have afforded to abandon it altogether. No, she intended to come back for it, to come back to Jesus with her friends.

How could she do otherwise? Considering Christ's unprecedented conversation with her in public, because his light exposed her darkness and his promise captured her heart, her passion for life was suddenly transformed. She became instantly earnest to introduce others—who also knew her past—to this man. She did not want to show them some new and exciting religion. Nor did she want to show them the error of their ways, or some nifty set of values that could magically make their lives better.

No, she became focused entirely on bringing the people in her life (probably even the lover with whom she was currently sleeping) to see the man who—of all things—showed her

her sin. She wanted them to meet the man who could be the Messiah, the long-awaited hope of people like her; indeed, the man who actually said, "I am he." After all, he had exposed her transgressions and revealed her true self; he had identified her thirst and revealed his nature for quenching it. In the process, she had seen both her sinfulness *and* his forgiveness and love as the Messiah, the bad news and the good news! He offered her true water that both cleansed and satisfied. And she got a glimpse of her true purpose: to worship the eternal God as the lady she was always meant to be.

She did not suddenly try to be someone she was not. She had simply tasted enough of the living water to know this would satisfy all of her thirsts. And if it could do that for her, surely it could do that for others. Like a beautiful song you can't help but want others to hear, she had to let others know about the prophet at the well.

And so she did. Not with a sermon or a formula but with a story and a question: "Come, see a man who told me everything I ever did. Could this be the Messiah?"

### The Counsel

What can we learn from the Samaritan woman at the well? What counsel does she give us? First, she came to the well to do one job, and after encountering Jesus she was given another. He was—and is—able to transform even the most mundane routine when we have eyes to see him alive and working in the moment. Second, though she talked of the physical and material world, he did not dismiss those issues as unimportant, but he used them to turn the conversation toward her deeper spiritual needs. So much so that he ended in a discussion of worship. Even as the disciples came back offering him physical food, he directed them instead to the spiritual. He offered them sustenance that nothing else would provide: himself.

An offer that still sings to us across the centuries.

But how? How could he do this? How was it possible for this man from Galilee to make such a claim? In fact, how could this young carpenter-turned-rabbi, this radical Jewish teacher who'd been born in a barn, make any of the claims he did in his interaction with this woman? Or in the words he gave to his disciples?

Because he knew who he was as God's Son—the second Person in the Almighty Trinity—and he knew his purpose, why he came to earth in the first place. He knew that he would soon enough hang on a cross for all of them and cry out, "I thirst!" He would take on their thirsts and longings and hungers so that they—so that we—would be filled with his abundant and sacrificial life.

As the Samaritan woman talked with the man who would thirst for her sake, she suddenly understood that she had *not* been doing what she was born for; instead—and this is another lesson—she was given a new but unique opportunity to worship God and to point others to him. She responded not by instantly becoming Sally Spiritual but by simply being herself, with her own personality and a redeemed sense of dignity.

She apparently went back to her people exactly as she had always been and told them honestly, "Come and see." She did not say to them, "You fellow sinners, you pagans, you idiots! Clean up your lives!" She only pointed them to Jesus and invited them to see for themselves. She was a lot like the fickle man known as Peter who became the Rock (as I say in my book *Reckless Faith: Living Passionately as Imperfect Christians*), who was called for a calling. She was called first to Jesus, and then as a result of who he was (and not what she did), she was given a whole new purpose to match her individual passion.

History suggests that after this single encounter at the well, there was nothing short of a revival in Samaria, largely because of the nameless woman's testimony (in verse 39). Which is another lesson we can learn: once we enter into a personal relationship with Jesus Christ, everyone around us is affected as well. She was invited to drink of the living water Jesus offered her not merely to meet her need but for a much bigger purpose—as we always are too.

Becoming a Christian (or a follower of Christ) has never only been about our own personal salvation. Contrary to popular American "theology," coming to Jesus is never about having him solve the problems of life. He is not a spiritual genie whose purpose is to make us happy, as if he owed us anything. No, entering a relationship with the God of the universe through Jesus Christ is never an idealistic or individualistic act, though it is a personal decision. Instead, it is about a bigger purpose, a bigger story, a bigger community known as the kingdom of God. In the process, Christ's life automatically pours out of ours into others, like yeast in dough.

But before the woman went back to her community to tell them about the prophet, did she first clean up her own life to "look" better? Did she become instantly holy and righteous when Jesus declared to her "I who speak to you am he"? Of course not. She acknowledged the reality that this man had accepted her as she was, affirmed her as the woman she was always meant to be, and so she simply, honestly, remained herself—only now she was fulfilled. Something inside her changed that day, enough so she could whisper, "My name is Dulcinea."

I bring out this point because I've known friends through the years who've told me they needed first to change their lives, to give up this unhealthy relationship or quit that bad habit, before they could become Christians. But the counsel from this story suggests otherwise; that if we'll simply say yes to the person of Jesus, then he can be trusted to take care of the rest. We do not know what happened to this woman and the men in her life once the Messiah had smitten her.

We only know his love made all the difference for her, and for her community of friends.

Considering all she'd lived through, how could she not respond to Jesus by telling her village about him? But notice she did not preach at her old friends, nor did she go on and on about Jesus, arguing with them or trying on her own ability to convince them of his truth. She simply went to them and pointed to Jesus. "Come and see," she said, implying that together they would go to the Messiah as equals, as friends, not as righteous and pagans, believer and unbeliever, but as fellow sinners in need of grace.

She was simply one thirsty soul telling another where to find a drink, one that would last.

## The Conversion

So her life was transformed, converted, and changed because of a "chance" encounter while doing a mundane task. Then her friends and neighbors were too. Not because she was doing anything spiritual or exceptional but because she had the humility to accept a spontaneous meeting with a man who told her who she was: a sinner with a past in need of a Savior who could offer her a future. That was the essence of their exchange and the truth of what she accepted. And certainly it was the worst, the best, and the most freeing news she had ever heard. Why?

Because now she would do what she was born for. *She* was the worshiper of whom he spoke, the fields that he had described to his disciples. *She* was the lovely outcast for whom he—like Don Quixote—would offer his heart and his life and would be willing—like Don Quixote—to "march into hell for a heavenly cause."[4] Why? So that she would become a lady, a woman of dignity with a kingdom purpose, one who had found in him what she had thirsted for all her life.

Yes, a woman with an intensely parched soul was changed—converted—into a woman of deep satisfaction, all because of the love of a man who would die a suffocating death on a cross for her sake, who would give up all that filled him to fill her. A man who invited her to forgo the other idols in her life to instead worship him, the living water, so that everyone who knew her would be affected.

The fountain spilled over again and again!

As it does still today. Because Christ is the same yesterday, today, and forever (see Heb. 13:8), his invitation to us now is as real as it was when he stopped at noon by the well in Samaria to chat with a woman whose name we don't know. He still seeks the type of worshipers who will worship him with spirit (passion) and truth (honesty), just as they are. He still seeks those women and men daring enough to admit that no other human, no idol, no achievement or any other thing can satisfy the passions of their hearts. Only the Living Water can make such a promise—and keep it.

Only he could fulfill the Scripture that the prophet Isaiah described:

> The poor and needy search for water, but there is none; their tongues are parched with thirst. But I the LORD will answer them; I, the God of Israel, will not forsake them. I will make rivers flow on barren heights, and springs within the valleys. I will turn the desert into pools of water, and the parched ground into springs. I will put in the desert the cedar and the acacia, the myrtle and the olive. I will set pines in the wasteland, the fir and the cypress together, so that people may see and know, may consider and understand, that the hand of the LORD has done this, that the Holy One of Israel has created it.
>
> 41:17–20

The call remains for us to, "Come and see." To come, as many other Christians throughout the ages have done, and drink deeply from the well of his salvation. To see the victory of his grace. Could this be, after all, the Messiah, the longing behind every longing we have?

# — In-Between Reflection —

1. After having read chapter 1, what new insights stand out to you about the story of the Samaritan woman at the well?

2. What struck you from the story of Don Quixote and Dulcinea?

3. The woman at the well is from Samaria. Why do you think this is an important detail in the story? Which part of the story from John 4 could you most relate to and why?

4. Jesus intentionally went to this woman and invited her into a relationship with him. In so doing, it changed her calling, even her very purpose in life. What effect does her new calling have, and how might this speak to you in your current vocational situation?

5. In what ways does the interaction between Jesus and the Samaritan woman change your view of the words *desperate* and *passion*?

6. How does the story of your own life reflect the truth of John 4:1–42?

# DIGGING DEEPER

All humans are thirsty for meaning, significance, and satisfaction. Often these needs are met through the gift of relationship and intimacy with our Creator and with his people. Examine the following verses in light of the story of the Samaritan woman at the well: Psalm 107:9, Isaiah 55:1, and John 19:28–29. What do they teach you about the metaphor of thirst and water?


Of the four Gospel writers, only John records the story of the Samaritan woman and of Christ on the cross saying, "I am thirsty." What else distinguishes John's Gospel and how does this affect your relationship with God?

# Preparation

*LUKE 13:10—17*

### A Crippled Woman Healed on the Sabbath

[10]On a Sabbath Jesus was teaching in one of the synagogues, [11]and a woman was there who had been crippled by a spirit for eighteen years. She was bent over and could not straighten up at all. [12]When Jesus saw her, he called her forward and said to her, "Woman, you are set free from your infirmity." [13]Then he put his hands on her, and immediately she straightened up and praised God.

[14]Indignant because Jesus had healed on the Sabbath, the synagogue ruler said to the people, "There are six days for work. So come and be healed on those days, not on the Sabbath."

[15]The Lord answered him, "You hypocrites! Doesn't each of you on the Sabbath untie his ox or donkey from the stall and lead it out to give it water? [16]Then should not this woman, a daughter of Abraham, whom Satan has kept bound for eighteen long years, be set free on the Sabbath day from what bound her?"

[17]When he said this, all his opponents were humiliated, but the people were delighted with all the wonderful things he was doing.

When you are ready, continue reflecting on the following question:

Perhaps you've read this story before. What new insights or observations jumped out to you as you read her story anew in this Gospel account? Jot them down. Take a few moments to reflect before reading chapter 2.

**Prayer:** *"May the power of your love, O Lord, fiery and sweet as honey, wean my heart from all that is under heaven, so that I may die for love of your love, You Who were so good as to die for love of my love."*

St. Francis of Assisi

---

2

---

# BENT, BATTERED, AND BROKEN

Her torso was bent forward, her body forever fused into a subtle question mark as her face angled toward the ground, hidden from the watchers at their windows.

They never saw the great dark eyes—the beauty of the beast.

Carol O'Connell, *Dead Famous*

When I was growing up in the foothills of Denver—Colorado's Mile High Capital—there weren't many days I stayed inside. Whether sledding in the snowy field behind our house, riding figure eights on my bike in the driveway when the lilacs were in bloom, or "camping" in the backyard on hot summer nights, I was a happier kid when I was outside. The older I got, the more I looked for opportunities to enjoy the great outdoors, especially to play soccer or tennis in the city, to ski or backpack in the Rockies. I was an active—though not particularly disciplined—athlete who simply loved to play. So much so that I expected to be "playing" until my hair turned gray and my teeth fell out.

Of course, life is rarely what we expect. And by my thirty-fifth birthday I began limping. A lot. I was still playing soccer on a coed recreational team but struggling more and more simply to walk off the field after each game. My cleats became harder to tie, my joints—particularly my left hip—became achy and stiff. Once I finally forced myself to visit the doctor, I got the bad news: I had advanced arthritis and would qualify immediately for a hip replacement. In fact, he told me, I would probably not make it to my fortieth birthday before being completely unable to walk normally.

The diagnosis was more of a blow to my ego and dreams than to my body, reminding me, as physical ailments always do, that I was not invincible, as my youthful Colorado attitude had led me to believe. Still, I would do what I needed to maintain my athletic lifestyle, if for no other reason than to spite the doctor who wanted to sell me a hip like it was a new car!

So for the next eleven years, I adjusted my life to fit my arthritic condition. I replaced jogging with bike riding, traded hiking for reading, and enjoyed the fireplace of the lodge instead of the moguls of the ski slopes. I'd kick around in a swimming pool when I could, take the occasional low-impact aerobics class, and eat more green and less white. I asked friends to pray for me and swallowed various vitamins to supplement their prayers, in hopes that either—or both—might "work" and I'd be healed. Though it's not very spiritual, I confess that I eventually gave up on divine intervention and simply accepted the fact that I was going to have to live with my arthritis. And I was always going to limp.

Granted, most of my feeble efforts did help for a while, but eventually nature ran its course. After one huge Christmas dinner a few years ago, I was out walking with my

Desperate Women of the Bible

husband's family when piercing bolts suddenly shot from my hip to my toes. My limp reflected the pain, my brow grimaced, and my sister-in-law asked the obvious: "So why don't you get that fixed? What are you waiting for?!"

*Courage,* I thought. I was waiting to become brave enough to subject myself to surgery for the first time in my life. I wasn't dumb; I knew they cut you in surgery and you bleed, neither of which were particularly appealing to me. Besides, I was also waiting for some amazing new technology that might replace my battered joint with no pain and less inconvenience. Or maybe I was still living in denial that my hip hurt at all, and when I did notice it, maybe I was really waiting for a miracle. Maybe I was waiting for the prayers to be answered.

Whatever my reasons for delaying the obvious and after one too many pain-filled nights and humiliating moments when my husband had to tie my shoes for me, I came to the end of myself. I became desperate for a change. I began to prepare. We found a leading orthopedic surgeon in New York City near our home, scheduled the date, and almost a year from that Christmas stroll we drove to the hospital. Five days later I came home with stitches in my skin, a new titanium and ceramic hip in my joint, and a whole new appreciation for the creativity of medical artists.

To think about it now, I can't believe I really went ahead with it, given my fears, aversion to pain, and lack of faith. I'm even more in awe that I live in a time when medical research has advanced to this place at all, when joints can be replaced, hearts can be bypassed, and cancer can be treated. I don't know why God placed me in the wealthiest nation on earth at this time in history, but sometimes I think it's because he knew I probably wouldn't have made it to fifty at any other time or place. He knows I'm a wimp.

Nonetheless, it's no small thing to enjoy walking normally again on the beach or a city sidewalk, to sleep comfortably through the night, or to bend over to tie my shoes again. Though I don't expect to play soccer any time soon or tackle any ski slope, my daily life is radically different today than it has been for the past twelve years. It's not an understatement or a cliché to say that I feel I have a new lease on life. I have. The miracle of health has been given to me again.

Restored.

## A Woman of Defect

And so when I read the story of another woman's crippled state, when I imagine what she endured for eighteen long years, I am all the more in awe of the consistent yet personal nature of the God of history. Luke 13:10–17 tells her beautiful story: how this nameless, disabled woman must have heard that a radical young rabbi would be teaching in the local synagogue on the Sabbath, and she figured it couldn't hurt—too much, anyway—to go. What she did not anticipate was that the rabbi would call her forward in front of all the religious gurus who'd also come to hear him that day.

It must have been the longest walk in synagogue history. But neither she nor most of those around her were disappointed.

We already know from our previous chapter that Jesus intentionally pursued a physically healthy but emotionally damaged Samaritan woman and willingly engaged in a lengthy chat with her that changed her life and the lives of her friends. Yet this story of an equally desperate but physically challenged woman yields a similar result through an entirely different exchange. In fact, their interaction includes far fewer words, though it is just as profound. And just as relevant for crippled bodies and souls (like ours) today.

## The Context

Before we look at her story, let's learn a bit about the man who recorded it since this story only appears in Luke's Gospel. Luke was an enormously talented man. A Gentile by birth and well-educated in Greek culture, he enjoyed a career as a doctor before accompanying the Jewish-convert preacher named Paul at various times on his missionary journeys until Paul first landed in a Roman jail. Luke remained a loyal friend of the apostle even after others deserted him. Unlike the disciple and writer John—who probably stumbled on the interaction with Jesus and the Samaritan woman at the well when he returned from town with the other disciples—Luke was not an eyewitness of Christ's ministry. In fact, he probably learned of the stories he recorded from Paul and others, which suggests he was also a natural investigative reporter. He obviously was intellectually curious and socially concerned, and consequently provided a unique perspective of Christ's culturally radical interactions with women and other marginalized individuals. Through Luke, we're given a rich perspective of Christ's time on earth. He knew how to pay attention to the firsthand "experts" on the subject of Jesus.

Theologians would characterize Luke's Gospel as the one that focuses mostly on the kingdom of God. Luke seemed to place a greater value on what has come to be called the Social Gospel than the other writers, that is, the justice and mercy issues integral to Christ's kingdom. Most agree that Luke was also the author of Acts, and many regard him as a writer's writer because of his command of language, attention to historical details, sensitive understanding of Jesus, and keen awareness of the issues of the day.

When we arrive at Luke 13:10–17, we know that Jesus was in the last year of his life, having created many enemies by now for making the claims he did. On this specific Sabbath day, he was teaching in someone else's synagogue, which, according to the times, meant it would have drawn a largely male crowd. If synagogues did allow women into the congregation, the women likely stood either way in the back or on the sides, keeping men in the center and the leaders up front. It's important to remember, too, that women were generally thought to be second-class citizens in both the wider culture and in Jewish circles and therefore, as Spurgeon said, "unfit for religious instruction." Jesus of course thought otherwise. And so as he was teaching on the Sabbath (as was the custom), a day when no other work was allowed (v. 14), he wouldn't have minded at all if a few women also took a break and crashed the service.

This was not necessarily true of the Jewish ruler who ran this particular synagogue. Though we don't know where he stood on gender issues, we do know that he was well versed in Jewish law. He knew the rules of his religion and believed a good rabbi would not venture outside those lines. Everything to him was clear cut, historic, and therefore unmovable, sacred even. So much so that to him, faith in God had become almost a robotic religion. If the Sabbath law, for instance, mandated that no one be permitted to do any active work on that sacred day, he would enforce it, as this passage shows. His belief system revolved around ultimate obedience to the ordinances of God so that God would see his holy life and bless him because of it.

Before we roll our eyes at the legalism of this strict religious leader, maybe we should look at our own lives. I know that I've often told God I'd do a righteous deed for him, believing it would establish some sort of spiritual "credit" for me I could later cash in on when I needed a specific blessing. How often have I asked for his favor—or his healing of a lame hip for that matter—as I promised then to be nice to my neighbor? Haven't we all tried to make deals with God and then became disappointed or, worse, disillusioned, if he didn't answer us as we wanted? But God would hardly be God if we thought he owed us something. Instead, if we're really honest with ourselves, it is we who see ourselves as gods if we think he should cater to our whims. Neither we nor this synagogue ruler deserve any blessing from the Almighty.

That's why it is called grace. Mercy made flesh.

Still, this man knew and observed the Jewish law. He knew enough to care for the poor, to observe the laws of the prophets, to say his prayers, and to lead his congregation. Nonetheless, his spiritual obedience or religious rhetoric hardly impressed the visiting rabbi known as Jesus. The great irony of the story of course is that this synagogue leader clearly understood that the Sabbath day was a day made for rest by God and was to be strictly observed. Yet he was so bound to his dogma that he could not relax in the presence of its Maker, even after he witnessed a great miracle!

To his credit, though, he was right when he said, "There are six days for work" (v. 14). Yes, a Sabbath rest is important, and Lord knows we could all use more of it! We absolutely need to stop at least once a week, to rest our spirits, focus our hearts, and direct our attention to the One who is behind all we do. It is no accident that the Creator of the universe ordained a day of rest for his people. When we observe the Sabbath by setting aside time out of our busy weeks, we fulfill our true purpose: worship. During such intentional times, we are refreshed, recharged, and redirected, ready to enter again the demands of daily life.

Yes, we need the Sabbath day God created for our own physical good and spiritual protection, just as the synagogue ruler implied we need restraints and boundaries whenever we gather to worship God. If we had neither, our lives and our worship would be full of chaos, disorder, and despair, exhausting us rather than nourishing us for the road ahead. In other words, the command to rest on the Sabbath day was just as important to obey in Christ's time as it is now. As a result, we need to help each other protect it.

Still, Jesus turned the old perception of the Sabbath rule on its head. He was angry that the ruler had made the gift of God's law more important than the Giver of the law. The ruler had elevated tradition above the One from whom tradition was derived, and by so doing, the synagogue leader actually missed the very presence of God in the moment. Then again, God's kingdom often turns people of faith upside down, challenging their expectations of what their belief systems should be like. Now Jesus was challenging the idolatry of the law, and even more radically, he was doing it by calling forward a crippled, bent-over, second-class citizen!

Make no mistake: the air in that synagogue must have been dripping with tension.

## The Conflict

Imagine it: a crippled, defective, imperfect, marginalized, poverty-stricken woman who couldn't even hold up her head to look Jesus or the synagogue leader in the eye found her way into the place. She came to listen, probably not expecting anything but simply to perform her religious duties. She likely joined the other women in the back and maybe a few young men who'd come to check out the visiting rabbi, most of whom probably either ignored her or steered clear of her because of her strange deformity.

The description Dr. Luke gave of this woman's infirmity suggested the bones of her spine were so rigidly fused together, shoving her shoulders so far forward to relieve the pain in her spinal cord, that she couldn't help but stare at the dirt with each step she took. The more she threw her shoulders forward to redirect the pain in her back, the more the joints fused together. It was an increasingly debilitating ailment that affected every aspect of her life. However, one part of the woman's health was not ailing: her hearing.

So when she heard the rabbi named Jesus call her forward, she might have needed an extra prodding from someone nearby, not because she could not hear his voice but because she did not expect to hear it. How could someone like him be calling someone like her? Apparently, though, she must have thought she had nothing to lose, and so with her heart beating out of her chest, her ears ringing from the heavy silence that came as she felt every eye in the temple watching her, she shuffled forward. Each step an effort. Each movement an agony. It was a long, slow walk.

But it was nothing she was not already familiar with. Luke tells us that for eighteen long years this woman was "crippled by a spirit." That meant eighteen years of an increasingly closer view of the dirt, of seeing the human filth, crusty feet, and animal dung that lined the primitive streets of the Galilean region where she lived. It was eighteen years of seeking any relief, of slowly forgetting what it was like to be normal, of reluctantly giving up hope. Suffering marked her life, and each day, each week, month, and year, she learned to adjust to the aching condition in her torso, to exist with it and rearrange her bones for the reprieve that never came. Nonetheless, regardless of her chronic and debilitating physical pain and the social alienation that inevitably came with it, this woman honored the Sabbath. In spite of the marginalized place to which her deformity had relegated her, still she came to the synagogue.

Something drove her. Some passion or desperation brought her to the temple.

Her own infirmity must have been amplified with the tension in the room between the local ruler and the visiting rabbi. Structure mandated that the synagogue ruler be responsible for conducting services, selecting participants, and maintaining order for the service, and because clearly no one had planned on the presence of this woman, the ruler was undoubtedly nervous as she shuffled forward. Jesus did not ask the synagogue ruler's permission to call her forward; he simply acted on his mission to restore people to their proper purpose.

But by calling this woman, touching her, and then confirming with his word that she was set free from her infirmity, he was establishing his authority over that of the ruler—or traditional law, for that matter. He was risking his reputation, his life, to release her from her pain. And as if his outright defiance of the synagogue custom was not enough to test the patience of the synagogue leader, the woman actually responded to Christ's words, straightening up and praising God, solidifying the ruler's rage. There was real trouble in the air.

Both Christ's unorthodox action and the woman's unbridled gratitude inconveniently disrupted the order of the Sabbath worship service and pushed all the buttons of its overseer. After all, any visiting preacher was expected to operate within the confines of tradition, and any participant in the service, let alone one who publicly praised the Maker of the universe, had to be chosen and approved. This woman had not been chosen to participate, if she had been noticed at all. Rules were rules, yet because of the radical healing extended by Jesus, this formerly crippled woman couldn't help dancing a holy jig before God and all these religious leaders! Everything was out of order.

In an effort to regain some control, the synagogue leader admonished the people (though he did not confront Jesus) for defying the Sabbath law, and in the process clearly tried to discredit the woman who was now standing upright, arms extended toward heaven. Jesus, of course, responded next by doing what he was sent to do: he defended the outcast and at the same time confronted the religious assumptions of the day with their own hypocrisies.

He knew the local leaders untied their ox or donkey to give them water or led them to the feeding trough even on the Sabbath in order to restore the animals for their original purpose: life and strength. In the same way, he chastised the leaders for ignoring the original purpose of the Sabbath: to restore. Why, then, should he not loose the chains from a woman whom Satan had bound for eighteen years so she could do what she was born to do: praise?

As Eugene Peterson said in *The Message*, "So why isn't it all right for me to untie this daughter of Abraham and lead her from the stall where Satan has had her tied these eighteen years?" Yes, the Son of Man knew that his touch would indeed restore and invite this woman—and all women and men—to do what God had designed them to do, to fulfill their original purpose on earth as worshipers of the one true God.

But such a touch, a word, a claim humiliated his adversaries, creating a growing tension between them. The crowd of other crippled souls, however—those who *knew* they were crippled, that is—"was delighted and cheered him on" (Message, Luke 13).

## The Counsel

What do the characters in this intense exchange teach us? What can we learn from them? What could we glean from a crippled but desperate woman, a marginalized female in the midst of a male-dominated religion, who was minding her own business, paying God respect on the Sabbath when she encountered a great rabbi in someone else's digs and a ruler whose authority was threatened by both? Why did Luke record this story at all?

First, because it happened. This once deformed woman really did stand up straight to praise God once Jesus touched her. A miracle? Absolutely. But it was more than simply a display of his power to heal a hurting woman, though of course that in itself ought to deepen our faith. The truth of this event ought to remind us that a perfect God invaded a vastly imperfect world, one full of tragically imperfect lives, so that he could bring some order and wholeness to these fragmented days. It reveals both Christ's power as God incarnate and his desire to relieve the marginalized of their suffering. The story of this crippled woman who straightens up to praise God ought to increase our faith and enlarge our vision that he is able to do far more than all we could ask or even begin to imagine.

Lord, help my unbelief.

But the story is about more than the gift of restoration. True, it revealed Christ's nature for the brokenhearted and broken-bodied souls of the world, but it also showed that he had enemies. In other words, throughout the Gospels as Jesus challenged the local authorities, as he brought God's kingdom by healing or multiplying or liberating or touching or preaching, he also helped usher in his own demise as a man. People did not necessarily like what he did or what he said (and still don't) or especially those with whom he chose to spend time. With each friend he made, a foe emerged.

Change was not easy for the humans in Christ's time on earth, just as it isn't now. Like the synagogue ruler, we don't like having our assumptions questioned, our expectations challenged, and our minds baffled by things we can't explain. That can be messy.

Yet, that's why Christ came to earth: to show us something better than life as we know it or believe it to be. And with each interaction, Jesus was well aware that he was coming closer to his ultimate purpose on earth. He was coming closer to the cross.

Jesus fulfilled the Sabbath law of rest in the synagogue because he knew he would be offering himself soon enough as the ultimate sacrifice for sins and defects so that we could rest in him. He was able to offer this crippled woman a second lease on life by healing her and restoring her broken body because he knew his body would be broken for all humanity. He could establish his authority over

Satan, sin, defects, and religious law because he knew he would give up his authority to endure the wrath of local officials so threatened by his power that they would sentence him to death. Jesus proclaimed this woman's freedom, touched her, restored her body and spirit to its original purpose—worship—because he would soon experience absolute bondage, utter loneliness, and excruciating suffering on the cross.

And he didn't stop there. He affirmed the identity of this previously obscure and nameless woman by now calling her a "daughter of Abraham" because he would put to death the old ways of existing to offer new life to her and countless others like her.

What can we learn from this story? Simply this: that we all come to the synagogue very aware of our own defects, shortcomings, inadequacies, and marginalization. They bog us down so that we can't even see straight or look up. But Jesus calls, at great personal cost to himself. When we respond, we're changed. And we cannot help but stand up and look toward heaven in praise.

### The Conversion

This woman went from being an anonymous outsider to a daughter of Abraham. What did she do to be noticed? Nothing. How did she get Christ's attention? By being broken, desperate, and present. Did she contribute in any way to the change she experienced? Only by hearing his call. She responded to Christ's invitation. She did not earn her way to salvation nor did she get healed before going to him. She did not let a fear of the crowd or the synagogue ruler keep her from going forward—she could not even see them, after all!

Did she know what was going to happen? Probably not. Did she have anything to lose? Not a thing. After eighteen long years, she was all too willing to take a few extra steps down the aisle in a synagogue.

And so a woman of defect became a woman of praise. A woman who couldn't even look at the sky became a woman of perspective because her focus now was on the Man who called her, who proclaimed her freedom, who dared to touch her broken body with his healing hands. How could she, how could we, not respond with praise?

And why praise him? Because she was restored for her own sake? Not only for her own life but for others, for us. She was not merely an isolated daughter, she was now a daughter of Abraham, brought into the family of God for the sake of the whole family. So too was she healed not just for her own sake but for the sake of those watching—either then or in the Scriptures now.

Every aspect of our lives affects other people. All of the gifts we receive are to serve others, pointing them to the Giver of all good things. As one commentary put it,

> The praise of God in the Psalter is rarely a private matter between the psalmist and the Lord. It usually is a public (at the temple) celebration of God's holy virtues or of his saving acts of gracious bestowal of blessings. In his praise the psalmist proclaims to the assembled throng God's glorious attributes or his righteous deeds. To this is usually added a call to praise, summoning *all* who hear to take up the praise, to acknowledge and joyfully celebrate God's glory, his goodness and all his righteous acts. This aspect of praise in the Psalms has rightly been called the Old Testament anticipation of New Testament evangelism.[1]

In other words, according to the Hebrew tradition, the very public act of someone standing up in the synagogue to praise God would naturally have called others to do the same, to invite the community around him—or her—to participate together in praising God for his wonders. It was a public and corporate display of gratitude for the demonstration of his sovereign lordship over the hard and real circumstances of living.

And so this broken, crippled woman really did become a woman who could stand up straight and honor her Maker. As she did, she indirectly invited others to join her in acknowledging the Man who could transform broken, meaningless existences into purposeful lives of dignity. In the same way, he calls us to come forward to him and to be changed so that we, too, will live lives of gratitude and praise.

What happens when we do? Others are drawn to our attitudes of thankfulness, and our joy becomes contagious. And in God's mercy, other people are automatically attracted to that place known as God's kingdom, where crippled bodies are restored, hearts are refreshed, and tired souls are invited to rest in the One who broke into our humanity with his grace.

That kind of good news is worth standing for.

# In-Between Reflection

1. For eighteen years, this woman was crippled, bent over, and unable to stand upright at all. Yet she managed to come hear Jesus in the synagogue on the Sabbath. What part of her story most connects with you? *the desire to hear a new voice - will this be the one to make a difference.*

2. How do you think the woman might have felt when Jesus called her forward in front of the crowd? Why do you think he spoke to her of his healing *before* he touched her? *She was probably surprised she would have been used to being ignored*

3. Note the difference between the synagogue leader and the woman in their responses to Jesus on this Sabbath day. One seemed bound by "rules" while the other was free to praise God. What other differences strike you? What new insights about Jesus, passion, and worship does this story inspire for you? *Jesus saw healing as part of worship not work!*

4. Can you remember a time when it was difficult for you to publicly worship God, to stand up straight and praise him for his kindness to you? Or to take the first step toward standing up for what was right? What happened? *It is still hard for me to not dwell on what is wrong - what I could have done differently*

5. Are there some areas in your life that might have kept you from "looking up" to praise God? Or perhaps you've experienced either physical or emotional pain. How has this kept you from cultivating an attitude of praise or thanksgiving? *I need to live more in the 'now' + be thankful for all I have*

6. What do you have to be thankful for today? How does reflecting on these things—and Christ's sacrificial love for *you*—change your perspective? *My family, my children + husband, my sister*

## DIGGING DEEPER

*what lease God is a humble heart*

All people are broken by sin and disabled in some capacity. Obviously, none of us is perfect, though we often want to believe otherwise. Yet we know that neither reality is God's ultimate desire for us. Examine the following verses in light of the story of the crippled woman in the synagogue: Psalm 51:17, Isaiah 53, and Luke 22:63–65. What does each suggest about the broken condition of humanity and God's redemption in Jesus? *The Lord after suffering he will see the light of life + be satisfied*

How does this give you new insight about the sacred act of communion during corporate worship?

# Preparation

MARK 12:35—44

## Whose Son Is the Christ?

35While Jesus was teaching in the temple courts, he asked, "How is it that the teachers of the law say that the Christ is the son of David? 36David himself, speaking by the Holy Spirit, declared:

> "'The Lord said to my Lord:
> "Sit at my right hand
> until I put your enemies
> under your feet."'

37David himself calls him 'Lord.' How then can he be his son?"

The large crowd listened to him with delight.

38As he taught, Jesus said, "Watch out for the teachers of the law. They like to walk around in flowing robes and be greeted in the marketplaces, 39and have the most important seats in the synagogues and the places of honor at banquets. 40They devour widows' houses and for a show make lengthy prayers. Such men will be punished most severely."

## The Widow's Offering

41Jesus sat down opposite the place where the offerings were put and watched the crowd putting their money into the temple treasury. Many rich people threw in large amounts. 42But a poor widow came and put in two very small copper coins, worth only a fraction of a penny.

43Calling his disciples to him, Jesus said, "I tell you the truth, this poor widow has put more into the treasury than all the others. 44They all gave out of their wealth; but she, out of her poverty, put in everything—all she had to live on."

When you are ready, continue reflecting on the following question:

Perhaps you've read this story before. What new insights or observations jumped out to you as you read her story anew in this Gospel account? Jot them down. Take a few moments to reflect before reading chapter 3.


**Prayer:** *"Dear Father, you who have given so much to me,*
*give one thing more, a generous heart. Amen."*

Bob Benson Sr., *Disciplines for the Inner Life*

---

3

---

# EMPTY POCKETS

The mystery of poverty is that by sharing in it, making ourselves poor in giving to others, we increase our knowledge of and belief in love.

Dorothy Day, *By Little and By Little*

The first time I ever experienced the intensely visual story entitled "Babette's Feast," I suddenly believed the world was a more delightful—and sensible—place. It is a powerful tale that led me to remember both the salty air of the sea and those extraordinary moments that happen around the dinner table with good friends. I even leaned back in my chair, closed my eyes for a moment, and sighed contentedly from the enchanting "meal" I'd just enjoyed. Yes, "Babette's Feast" was food for my soul.

But it wasn't until years later when I rented the video version that I realized I had never actually *seen* the Danish film nor read the story. I read the video jacket and was baffled: how was I already so familiar with this story without ever

---

having watched it? When I popped it into the VCR and saw the stark images, why did I suddenly have that feeling I'd seen this before, even though I knew I hadn't? Intrigued, I began watching and somehow I knew the story in a way one knows an old friend.

When the movie ended, I scrolled through my memory until finally it dawned on me: a few years before, I had checked out one of those books on tape from the library, listened to the choice language and finely crafted story as I made a long-distance trip in my car, and apparently digested its beauty so thoroughly I was certain I had been to this table before. In other words, the vivid details of "Babette's Feast" had rung so clearly in my ears that they formed lasting pictures in my mind. Not to mention an endearing affection for the characters and themes.

Maybe that is because "Babette's Feast" is first of all a literary treat. The short story by Danish writer Isak Dinesen (aka, Karen Blixen, best known for her memoir-turned-movie *Out of Africa*) first appeared in *Ladies Home Journal*, was then published in Dinesen's 1958 book, *Anecdotes of Destiny*, and went on to become a favorite morsel from her collective works of fiction and nonfiction. Shaped by a gifted writer who twice flirted with the Nobel Prize for Literature and earned the admiration of writers as diverse as Ernest Hemingway, Carson McCullers, and Truman Capote, Dinesen's funny little story had all the requirements of a great cinematic retelling. So when Danish filmmaker and screenwriter Gabriel Axel made it into a film in 1986, not many who had read the story were surprised that it went on to earn an Oscar that year as Best Foreign Film and a British Academy Award.

Not bad for a story about religious piety and really good food.

"Babette's Feast" is set in Dinesen's native coastal region of Denmark. Two devoted sisters give up personal romance and aesthetic pleasures to carry on the religious work that their father—who has since died—began in the small fishing village where they live. Theirs is a hard life, made harder from trying to lead the small pious community through the dull but sincere rituals their founder taught them.

When a stranger—a French woman known as Babette—arrives at their door in the middle of a storm, the sisters give her refuge. And Babette spends the next several years repaying them for their kindness by working as their house servant, cooking for the sisters and their community what they have eaten all their lives: boiled fish stew and ale bread. Their daily meal is not unlike their daily spirituality: bland, tasteless, and always the same.

But Babette has a secret that soon challenges both their religiosity and their appetites. When she learns she has won a French lottery back home, she asks the sisters if they would allow her to prepare a special memorial dinner for them to celebrate the anniversary of their late father's passing. She suggests inviting everyone in the religious community to partake, and reluctantly—for they are women of simple means—the sisters agree. Babette makes the long journey back to France to order all she will need and has the greatest of foods shipped home with her as she returns to the Danish coast. Then Babette, like an artist, spends the next several days preparing.

What happens next is what always happens whenever extravagant grace is served: resurrection. An extraordinary meal brings back the gifts of spiritual vigor and human sensuality. Though the community skeptically sits down at the table, they eventually stop their bickering, let go of their boredom, and for the first time in their lives experience tastes, smells, and flavors they never even knew existed. Instead of the fish stew and ale bread, they savor turtle soup, quail, wines, pastries, and fruits. And they stagger home giddy from the feast.

Babette is exhausted—but in that delightful way that comes from sacrificing all you have in order to give all you know you're capable of giving. The sisters are dumbfounded by the meal Babette has served, and when they question her, they finally learn what she'd been hiding all along: she'd once been the most famous chef in all of France, but when the political tensions of the Revolution grew, her husband and son were killed, leaving her widowed, poor, and without a kitchen. Desperate, Babette had sought refuge through a friend who'd once visited the sisters, and he sent her to them, knowing she'd be safe in this village where nothing ever changed.

Then the sisters learn another remarkable truth: Babette had spent all she won from the lottery—money that could have bought her an entirely new life—on the one meal she'd just prepared for them.

Beyond the culinary delights, I have always loved this nuanced and beautiful story that marries Christian faith and radical generosity with exquisite creativity. It reminds me that perhaps the highest calling we can heed—even the highest form of worship—is to embrace all of what it means to be human. Of giving all we have for the holiest of pleasures, the joy of offering our gifts for a greater purpose.

Imagine, then, the sympathy I felt when I learned the sad irony of the story's creator, Karen Blixen, a writer who apparently never learned the secret behind her heroine's joy. Blixen battled a lifetime of physical illnesses, lost loves, and severe career disappointments and literally died of malnutrition. Blixen's soul was perpetually poverty stricken; she knew neither the sincere faith of the sisters in her story nor the sacrificial joy exhibited in Babette's character. Her desperation never moved her beyond despondency.

In spite of her tragic demise, though, there can be no mistaking the wonder of her amazingly visual story—whether you watch it, read it, or listen to it. It points us to a greater story of another feast. And it reminds all who are familiar with biblical literature of another widow in another time who gave all she had for a purpose much higher than her own.

## A Woman of Lack

Obviously, the story of this nameless and sacrificial widow—found in both Luke's and Mark's Gospels—is as famous for its simplicity of purpose as it is for its inspiration behind countless other acts of generosity. We know it as the story of the widow's mite or the widow's offering; that is, of the husbandless woman who dropped two small, pathetic coins into the money box in the temple courtyard as Jesus, the Lord of the universe, looked on. It is a story that has been told and retold countless times, one about which—as I discovered once I began researching it—everyone seems to have an opinion.

Some believe this is not really a story about a poor widow as much as it is a story about greedy and wealthy religious leaders, as if the possession of money and the misuse of finances by spiritual leaders is the ultimate sin in a hierarchy of shortcomings. Some, on the other hand, see this story not as a rebuke to the wealthy but as a warning to vulnerable believers who make poverty seem like the highest spiritual calling there is. It "tempts" Christians, the thinking goes, to make the grave and irresponsible mistake of giving away all they own to enter some sort of ascetic, pleasureless existence for the kingdom of heaven. Still others claim it is a story that justifies invasive privileges for church boards to monitor the private tithes and offerings of individuals, publicly exposing the very amount each member gives to their church.

But like all stories with Jesus, it is more than all of these interpretations combined. And, of course, it is bad news before it is good news, news which soon evolves into that fairy tale that seems too good to be true. For first we have to look at the truth of history, that there really was a very poor widow (a female) who lived among some very greedy religious leaders (all males) in ancient Jerusalem. They had vastly contrasting lifestyles, both of which were probably the result of corporate injustices and cultural abuses.

But then there was also this popular young rabbi who visited the temple during the busiest time of the year with his buddies, sitting on a bench, watching and pointing and lecturing on the quirks and qualities of the people who passed them. He was a Jewish carpenter who'd been born in a stinky barn and now was poking holes in the religiosity of the elitists around him.

Then he actually had the chutzpah to notice this poor widow, this desperate woman, and call her nothing short of a hero. A model of sorts, he said, an example that far surpassed that of the leaders he'd just criticized.

This same curious guy was sensitive to things like this, because he himself was about to become poor so that all these misfits might become rich; he was about to offer all he had so stodgy old folks could someday sit down around a banquet table and stagger home giddy.

Yes, the story of this desperate widow communicates all of these elements of the Gospel story and ultimately shows us that it is in our lack that we learn the most about true wealth. This widow's story has much to offer, for as Edith Deen says in her book *All of the Women of the Bible*,

> The cash value of her gift compared to the gifts of the wealthy was hardly enough to notice, but the devotion behind it was another matter. That devotion, beginning there and spreading throughout the world, has built hospitals and helped the needy, fed the hungry and encouraged the imprisoned. Today the world knows more about the poor widow than about the richest man in Jerusalem in her day.[1]

### The Context

It was a busy time in Jerusalem—the annual Feast of the Jews—when Jesus was teaching in the synagogue with his disciples. In fact, it was the final Passover week of his earthly life. Knowing he was in his last days on earth, he wanted to make the most of his opportunities with his friends, and without a doubt this was one of the most teachable moments in all of Scripture.

First, like Luke, Mark was not an eyewitness of Christ's life. But he was a faithful friend and traveling companion of one of Christ's most famous disciples, Peter. Mark listened well to Peter—the flamboyant, impulsive, cocky fisherman-turned-humble-minister of the gospel—as Peter recounted the story of his Savior and friend, Jesus Christ, God Incarnate. Yes, Mark paid attention as Peter conveyed the details of Christ's interactions with various crowds, religious leaders, and, of course, marginalized women. Peter was likely with Jesus at the temple, so he too would have seen this widow as she dropped her pennies into the offering box. However, I suspect Peter—like most of us—would not have *noticed* her in the same way Jesus did. And he—like all of us—would not have elevated her to the status that Jesus did.

That's why the context of this passage becomes crucial in understanding what Jesus has done. It is true that Jesus had just been teaching on the hypocrisy and greed of the scribes and leaders. Many religious leaders were well aware of their responsibility to care for the poor and the outcast, but since they did not take a salary from the synagogue, they were also dependent on the gifts of the people. If the finances got a little low one week, it was not uncommon for some to go dipping into particular accounts that were designated for other ministries, like helping widows. Likewise, it was not uncommon for these same leaders to claim the best seats in the house of God and schmooze with successful businessmen in the marketplace. So it was not at all a surprise to the people listening that Jesus would have brought up the subject of greed among religious leaders. Everyone knew he was right on the mark.

As Jesus pointed out the superficiality of their religious rituals—walking around in flowing robes, making lengthy prayers—his followers no doubt were struck by his courage. Perhaps they knew all too well how easy it was to be trapped in customs of piety. Like the sisters whom Babette served, both the synagogue leaders and Christ's followers probably were sincere in believing their rituals were gaining spiritual points for them. But by verse 40 in Mark 12, Christ's displeasure with these leaders becomes so passionate that he had to speak out, "They devour widows' houses. . . . Such men will be punished most severely."

Obviously, shallow spirituality did not impress Jesus. A religious value system that revolved around "do's and don'ts" also didn't catch his attention. Neither did the wealth of those who had stopped by the treasury in the synagogue's courtyard. What caught Christ's eye was not the slick CEO nor the powerful politician who were dropping in wads of money from their already fat bank accounts. It was not the philanthropist who'd amassed millions through some clever entrepreneurial endeavor and now wanted to give to worthy causes to appease his conscience. The rich never seemed to win Christ's favor—just because they were rich, that is. Jesus didn't seem to care how deep their pockets were. Instead, it seemed as if he had a particular soft spot for those who lived on the other side of the tracks, who lacked the daily resources most mid-to-upper-class citizens took for granted.

To punctuate his point, Jesus decided to wander into what would have been known as the temple treasury, that rare public place where men and women could venture together because it was strategically located in what was called the Court of the Women within the Court of the Gentiles. The area contained thirteen trumpet-shaped receptacles for contributions brought by worshipers.

Women were welcomed, encouraged even, to enter this area in order to give their money to the work of God. But they were rarely, if ever, allowed to go into the temple to receive (or give) any spiritual blessing or religious instruction, or to extend any demonstration of praise to their Maker. Their role was clearly defined and relegated to a space associated with the economic contributions of worshipers, not the spiritual. Women could offer their money for the work of God, but not their talents or their worship.

Nonetheless, because it was a busy time for the God-fearing residents and visitors of Jerusalem, Jesus was taking full advantage of the situation. When he finished his sermon in the temple, he noticed dozens of men and women passing him, making their way to one of the trumpet-shaped offering boxes. As he stood with his followers, Jesus suddenly noticed a woman who apparently was as conspicuous in her lack as the others were in their wealth.

No doubt she had the appearance of poverty. Perhaps she wore rags, her face was dirty, or her hair matted. Perhaps she was attractive and well groomed, though wearing a battered dress. We don't know. We only know that the Lord immediately recognized her as a "poor widow." He noticed her. Because she was probably alone, which could have signaled her unmarried status, she was likely at a point of desperation, of need, of sheer lack. Yet, this passionate woman had managed to hang on to a thread of personal dignity and spiritual respect; otherwise I doubt she would have come to the synagogue at all. If she had been completely hopeless, she would not have yielded her offering into the holy box. She was desperate, but she was not despondent.

The leaders of the time had little patience for the poor—though they did not mind taking their money. The poor in turn gave out of fear and what little honor they had left, probably believing their meager offering could perhaps buy God's favor, or at least the favor of the men who ran the town. Neither, of course, was as God intended, and so the young radical rabbi who'd just delighted the crowds with his words, who'd just offended the prominent leaders of the time with his accusations, and who was just about to give one of the gloomiest end-times sermons in his ministry, shifted his focus now to the lines of people digging in their pockets.

Enter a displaced person in the middle of a storm. Things were about to get interesting.

## The Conflict

In the midst of a sexist and hypocritical culture, during a time of holy honor offered by sinful souls, in a place where the rich ruled and the poor had no hope of change, Jesus went to press some flesh in the slipperiest slope of the synagogue: the place where money was given and taken. He stood and he watched. His friends gathered around him, and they waited.

When a shuffling, marginalized widow got to her place in line at the offering box, she paused for a second and scrounged through her pocket. She did not find loose change there—she found all the money she had in the world. It was her savings, her retirement, her social security, her grocery account, and her rent all rolled into one. Only problem was it was only two coins—two measly pennies, or *lepta* in the Greek, which was a Roman copper coin worth about $\frac{1}{64}$ of a denarius, the same as a day's wage. She had no back-up plan, no credit card, no distant relatives to send a check next week, and no IRA account to dip into. This was it. Period.

Meanwhile, the rich guys, the fat cats, chuckled and waddled through the line, dropping their rolls of bills into the boxes. They tossed in their checks, their coins, their money, knowing they'd be getting paid again next week, knowing their savings accounts were earning interest, confident their inheritance was growing bigger and bigger. It didn't cost them a thing to give. But for anyone who was poor, especially a woman who had no husband to support her, it cost everything to give even a penny. Let alone two.

Which is why Jesus said she gave all she had. He knew her status, her economic condition, her destitution. And he knew who was running the place, why a woman like this was unlikely to see any return on her spiritual investment. He knew just who would be taking her money—the same leaders he'd just chastised for their superficial acts and unjust ways. And he knew from watching what the others were giving—and not giving—why this simple act was so extraordinary. He also knew what they were keeping. From what he could tell, this woman—this second-class citizen who had lost her husband—had kept nothing for herself. She gave all she had for what she believed was the work of God.

When a woman is desperate, she cannot help but feel vulnerable, defenseless, and exposed. She's out of control, in danger even, living solely at the mercy of others. Desperate living requires risk, surrender, yielding all that you have in hopes that it will somehow be good enough. It is jumping off of a cliff, hoping you will land on something soft, something that doesn't break you completely. Something that does not swallow you alive. But if it does, well, it does. To be desperate is to abandon any sense of security. It is trusting there is something bigger at work even when you have no obvious reason to believe it is so.

This widow was a woman who was jumping off of a cliff, clinging to the simple and frail hope that she might land on something soft—if she landed at all. While the others could rest in the temporary—and dare I say, illusionary—security of their salaries, this woman's entire survival was at stake. It was possible she might not make it out alive.

And that was exactly what Jesus noticed between her and the others: the contrast of the two types of offering. They gave and kept comfortably, responsibly, easily, because they could. She gave and kept irrationally, extravagantly, painfully because she had nothing else to fall back on. She did not know what she would eat that night for dinner. Or if she would eat at all. But still she gave. And she kept nothing.

What drove this poor widow to spend all she had so others could sit down to dinner?

## The Counsel

Somehow this woman—and I've known similarly generous women of limited economic resources—believed the higher calling for her was the work of God. It was not providing for herself but rather trusting in the reality that if she obeyed God's law to give, God would provide. It was enjoying the riches of a faith so deep that she could drop her last two coins in the offering plate and somehow believe things would work out.

In other words, this woman lived with her palms open and her fingers spread out wide. She held on tightly to nothing material, nothing earthly, because somehow this life was not all she had. There was something more. There were riches beyond this world that would satisfy more than all the bank accounts, stock investments, retirement plans, and professional salaries this world had to offer, combined. She was a woman whose devotion to the things of God seemed greater than that of any religious leader in Jerusalem during Holy Week.

Certainly, her story has much to offer on many levels. But I don't think Luke and Mark included it in their Gospels because they believed all Christians in all cultures should embrace poverty and renounce wealth—although it certainly wouldn't hurt western Christians to rethink what it means to live within our means and not according to our wants. (But that's another story!) Nor do I believe it is included merely

Desperate Women of the Bible

as a lesson about the haves and the have-nots of ancient Israel—although we are certainly called to care more than most of us do about daily realities of economic justice.

First, they included the interaction of the widow and her offering because it really happened. Jesus really was disgusted by the arrogance and abuse of the greedy leaders he'd confronted. Which was perhaps why this woman's humble gift was so noticeable to him. It was vastly different from the attitudes or actions of those who were supposed to be leading the flocks of Israel. In other words, this widow served up an altogether different meal.

But we must not see this so much as the story of a generous but poverty-stricken woman whose name we don't even know, but as a story that points us more to the Person of Jesus Christ. So what do we learn about him from this passage?

If we haven't already noticed this, Jesus was not impressed with the external possessions of an individual and was much more concerned with the internal matters of a person's heart. Because he was with the Father from the beginning, he also knew this world was only a blip in terms of eternity. No matter how rich we are, we can only bring our souls with us into eternity. No robe, no house, no earthly status can go with us once we breathe our last physical breath.

So in this encounter, Jesus revealed to us that outward actions, behaviors, and deeds reflect what really goes on in the heart of a man or woman. He had just renounced the superficial behavior of the scribes and synagogue rulers for the fact that their deeds betrayed the true purposes of their faith. Such actions communicated more about their insecurities and shortsighted vision than their eternal perspective or respect for the Hebrew Scriptures, around which their religion revolved.

By contrast, Jesus loved the humble but real devotion of the widow and despised the ostentatious piety the leaders displayed. He loved the seemingly reckless abandon of this woman's faith and abhorred the pretense of independent provision the rulers thought they had. Hers was a faith working through an honest love for and belief in the God of Israel, while theirs was a hollow religion, masked by rituals but emptied of any spiritual content. Jesus held her up as the example because she believed beyond her means. The scribes he chastised for exploiting women like her for their own selfish gain.

By holding up this otherwise anonymous widow as an example, it was as if Jesus were saying to us, "Live large! Give radically! Take risks! Sacrifice joyfully! I love it each time you do!" Maybe he even went a step further, implying that we will experience more of who he is each time we let go, that we will get to know him better as our faithful God and Provider each time we hand over all that we have.

How could he affirm such an act? How could Jesus encourage such "irresponsible" giving? Because he, the Son of God, knew that this widow's generosity was ultimately pointing to another sacrificial offering he was going to make very soon. He would take on her poverty—indeed the poverty of every human soul—to offer us the riches of his Father's eternal love. He was about to jump off a cliff, knowing nothing was going to break his fall.

Nothing, that is, but the object of his devotion, of his sacrifice. Of his love.

### The Conversion

The Gospel writers do not give us details of what happened to this woman after Jesus's public display of admiration for her. Nor do we know how the disciples responded, if their levels of generosity suddenly increased or if the synagogue funds suddenly broke a new record.

We do know that this woman had a sense of God's provision that she wanted to respond to him with sincere devotion and sacrificial giving. Her heart had already been won over by the idea of his greatness and the measure of his omnipotence. In some ways, I think it's even safe to say she was desperate for him, passionate for his work to continue, moved to give back to the One who had first given to her. In spite of all the cultural injustices and religious hypocrisies, this woman still believed that God was alive and involved with his people. No matter how many times the scribes "devoured the widows' houses" she still believed that the corporate gathering of God's people was the most worthy cause she could give to. So much so that she gave all she had and kept nothing.

Because of Christ's radical generosity to us, we cannot help but be moved to give of our gifts, our talents, our money, and our lives to the higher purposes of his kingdom. He longs for our devotion and invites us to participate with him in an eternal feast of life, one full of flavors and tastes and scents we never even knew existed.

This widow's simple act, and Christ's observation of it, has in fact inspired countless movements of radical generosity and extravagant deeds of grace throughout the history of the world. And even now, it gives new meaning to the favorite old psalm, "Taste and see that the LORD is good; blessed is the [wo]man who takes refuge in him" (Ps. 34:8).

# In-Between Reflection

1. What struck you about Babette's character and her feast? (You might consider checking out the video or reading the short story to appreciate it anew.)

2. No doubt you'd heard the story of the widow and her mite many times before. What new insights surfaced for you as you read it this time?

3. How would you define poverty and how would you define wealth?

4. How does this woman's example speak to you today? Why do you suppose Jesus held her up as an example to his followers?

5. What are some specific and creative ways you could consciously seek opportunities to give more generously?

6. What does it mean for *you* to "Live large! Give radically! Take risks! Sacrifice joyfully!"?

7. What does this story teach you about Christ's sacrifice for you?

## Digging Deeper

All of us are born into the world with nothing, and we take nothing with us when we pass on. Yet we spend the in-between time trying to accumulate things and wealth, often expecting them to give our lives meaning or joy. Certainly, God's blessings in provision are real, as is his desire for us to care for one another with those material blessings. But they cannot define us. Examine the following verses in light of the story of the widow and her mite: Proverbs 14:21, Isaiah 58, and 2 Corinthians 8:9. What does each teach you about poverty, riches, and God's concern for the poor?

What other verses can you find on these themes, and how can you live them out in radical ways with Christ's help?

# Preparation

## A Dead Girl and a Sick Woman

[21]When Jesus had again crossed over by boat to the other side of the lake, a large crowd gathered around him while he was by the lake. [22]Then one of the synagogue rulers, named Jairus, came there. Seeing Jesus, he fell at his feet [23]and pleaded earnestly with him, "My little daughter is dying. Please come and put your hands on her so that she will be healed and live." [24]So Jesus went with him.

A large crowd followed and pressed around him. [25]And a woman was there who had been subject to bleeding for twelve years. [26]She had suffered a great deal under the care of many doctors and had spent all she had, yet instead of getting better she grew worse. [27]When she heard about Jesus, she came up behind him in the crowd and touched his cloak, [28]because she thought, "If I just touch his clothes, I will be healed." [29]Immediately her bleeding stopped and she felt in her body that she was freed from her suffering.

[30]At once Jesus realized that power had gone out from him. He turned around in the crowd and asked, "Who touched my clothes?"

[31]"You see the people crowding against you," his disciples answered, "and yet you can ask, 'Who touched me?'"

[32]But Jesus kept looking around to see who had done it. [33]Then the woman, knowing what had happened to her, came and fell at his feet and, trembling with fear, told him the whole truth. [34]He said to her, "Daughter, your faith has healed you. Go in peace and be freed from your suffering."

³⁵While Jesus was still speaking, some men came from the house of Jairus, the synagogue ruler. "Your daughter is dead," they said. "Why bother the teacher any more?"

³⁶Ignoring what they said, Jesus told the synagogue ruler, "Don't be afraid; just believe."

³⁷He did not let anyone follow him except Peter, James and John the brother of James. ³⁸When they came to the home of the synagogue ruler, Jesus saw a commotion, with people crying and wailing loudly. ³⁹He went in and said to them, "Why all this commotion and wailing? The child is not dead but asleep." ⁴⁰But they laughed at him.

After he put them all out, he took the child's father and mother and the disciples who were with him, and went in where the child was. ⁴¹He took her by the hand and said to her, "Talitha koum!" (which means, "Little girl, I say to you, get up!" ). ⁴²Immediately the girl stood up and walked around (she was twelve years old). At this they were completely astonished. ⁴³He gave strict orders not to let anyone know about this, and told them to give her something to eat.

When you are ready, continue reflecting on the following question:

Perhaps you've read this story before. What new insights or observations jumped out to you as you read her story anew in this Gospel account? Jot them down. Take a few moments to reflect before reading chapter 4.

**Prayer:** *"O God, the source of all health: So fill my heart with faith in your love, that with calm expectancy I may make room for your power to possess me, and gracefully accept your healing, through Jesus Christ our Lord. Amen."*

The Book of Common Prayer

---

---

4

---

# REALLY SICK
# AND REALLY TIRED

I have never been anywhere but sick. . . . In a sense sickness is a place, more instructive than a long trip to Europe,
and it's always a place where there's no company, where
nobody can follow. Sickness before death is a very appro-
priate thing and I think those who don't have it miss one
of God's mercies.

Flannery O'Connor, *The Habit of Being*

On a hot summer night in the early 1980s, I wandered into
a coffeehouse in downtown Denver. By day, the place—a
long storefront room in an old office building—served as
an outreach center to the hundreds of homeless women
and men who'd been hit hard by the recession. But by
night, tables, folding chairs, coffee, tea, and candles transformed the space, offering emotional and spiritual reprieve
to anyone who found his way into this urban refuge. Always there was a musician or two who would bring a

guitar and pluck out an array of folk tunes, songs from the activist music of the 1960s (like Bob Dylan) that spilled into the pop era of the 1970s (like James Taylor). Anyone could wander in from the hard summer streets for some semi-decent live music, almost fresh coffee, and usually friendly conversation. If nothing else, it was a safe place to rest your bones.

In those days, I was a new but zealous follower of Jesus Christ and a wannabe Joni Mitchell, barely out of college and ready to help change the world. So with my mahogany Guild six-string guitar and my passionate—but very suburban—faith, I offered my limited talents to the Refuge once or twice a month. On this Friday night, I arranged myself on a bar stool behind a small microphone and began to strum the only songs in my repertoire thus far: John Denver "classics" and Jesus praise songs.

Usually, as I made my musical trek to the urban coffeehouse, I'd bring along a friend or two, sometimes even a few students from the suburban high school where I was teaching English. It was an adventure for all of us, leaving the familiar confines of our homogenous upper-middle-class neighborhoods for the wild diversity that city life always seemed to draw. We'd make the drive down Colfax Avenue to the heart of the Capitol area with fear, excitement, and naiveté battling in our bellies.

For this particular Friday night, a college friend had decided to join me. Carol had earned her nursing degree and was one of those naturally inclined caregiver types who'd also come recently to faith. We parked out in front of the office building as the sun was setting behind the Rockies. We laughed as we walked inside and set up. Carol found a seat in the back of the coffeehouse, near the door and the coffee table. I settled onto my bar stool and began to strum.

Within a half hour, all types of people had piled into the place. Neighbors and volunteers from a local church sat next to a few old friends of mine who'd come to offer moral support to me and to the mission of the center. A dozen or so folks from the streets sat scattered around the room, holding garbage bags of clothing or recyclable cans near them and staring at nothing in particular as they sipped their cups of sugar and coffee. Mostly, these homeless women and men stayed to themselves, chatting only when they needed another cup or an empty seat. I moved from "Country Roads" to "God Is So Good," offering a mediocre blend of background "noise" for this liquor-less lounge and urban shelter.

Halfway through the song "Jesus, Name above All Names," I saw a man stagger in at the back of the room. Carol noticed him too. He wore a couple of soiled army jackets—one on top of the other—blue-black jeans, and beat-up boots. His long black hair was matted and knotted as it hung over his shoulders. There was no focus in his eyes and no emotion on his face. Only dirt, pain, and blood.

I strummed. I watched the man slump into a chair and stare at the floor as I sang the chorus from behind my microphone and guitar. The people at his table got up and moved. He lifted his head slightly as they did, and I saw a long, deep cut across his forehead. Dried blood was caked around it. The man scratched it for a second before dropping his hand again in his lap. He coughed. Then he looked at me—I suppose simply because I was in his line of vision—nodded, and closed his eyes.

I swallowed and kept playing, though I was sure by now I was all but gawking at the poor man who'd just drifted in from some private war zone. So I did the only thing I could think of at the time: I segued into "This Is the Day."

I was in the middle of the line "that the Lord has made" when Carol got up from her seat across the room. I watched as she wove in and out of tables and talkers, focused in one single direction until she finally arrived where she wanted to be: in front of the man in the army coats, with dried blood smeared across his forehead.

"I will rejoice, I will rejoice and be glad in it," I sang as I watched Carol then do a most amazing thing: she leaned over the man—who opened his eyes as she did. She pushed her eyebrows forward like she was concentrating and moved her fingers gently along the cut on his forehead. He looked up at her, but he did not move or say a word. He seemed too tired. Next, Carol stood up straight, placed her hands on her hips, and shook her head from side to side as if she was impressed by the size of the wound.

I transposed my way into "Praise the Name of Jesus" while Carol hurried over to the sink by the coffeepots. She found a clean white towel, cradled it back and forth under the faucet, and hurried back to the man. She lifted his chin toward her, his blank gaze a stark contrast to her intensity, and she began to dab the cut with the towel until the towel turned a sort of rust color. With the calm of a surgeon, she washed each portion of the wound as the man simply stared into her face.

"He's my rock, he's my fortress," I sang, more on auto-pilot than from adoration. I was more absorbed by the story unfolding in front of me. While most of the other folks in the coffeehouse were sipping, or chatting, or laughing, Carol had returned to the sink, rinsed out the towel, and come back to the man's forehead within seconds, putting the finishing touches on his gouge. Behind my verses and guitar, my eyes followed as she darted across the room and back again. Then she reached into her purse, found a few Band-Aids (what nurse doesn't carry a mini first-aid kit?), and taped them across the man's cut, patting his shoulder to punctuate her diagnosis. He would be all right.

All without saying a word.

By the time I'd finished the last of the songs I knew Carol had returned to her seat. She was sipping her coffee while the man she'd just cared for had fallen fast asleep at his table, his head cupped on the back of his chair, his mouth wide open. He stretched out his beat-up boots far in front of him and dropped his hands at his sides while he slept. Someone offered Carol a piece of pie, and she bit into it as if nothing had happened. As if no great miracle had just occurred. As if cleaning the wound of a tired, dirty, homeless man was a normal part of life.

I knew better. From my bar stool and microphone, I'd just witnessed the Good News of the Gospel—live and up-close in downtown Denver in the middle of a hot summer night around cups of coffee and sugar.

The Word became flesh and dwelled among us.


## A Woman of Pain

To this day, my friend Carol has absolutely no memory of that exchange. When I push her, she recalls coming to the urban coffeehouse and hearing me sing (poor girl!) but for the life of her, she cannot remember the man or the cut or the cleansing of his bloody wound when I describe it to her. She remembers our youthful zeal for Jesus on the streets of Denver, and she can still sing along to all the folksy songs we belted out in those days. But Carol simply does not have an image in her head of an exhausted homeless man with matted hair and blood on his forehead.

I can't forget it. The picture of Carol cleaning the blood off of that man's face has never left me. It continues to move me and challenge me to think hard about caring for those people I'd never otherwise consider caring for. The untouchables, if you will, whose pain and despair and weariness from the misfortunes of life are often too much to bear. Friends who are social workers and nurses witness such human sorrow daily yet find great joy and mutuality in the privilege of serving those in need.

Though all Christians are indeed invited to care for those who cannot care for themselves—the poor, the destitute, the sick, the widows, and the orphans—I confess, I am not very good at this part of building God's kingdom. I want to be. Justice and mercy are constant voices in my head, though I rarely know how to listen to them. Often I cry at the images on the news of hurricane survivors or war victims. But just as often I feel too far away to help and too comfortable to respond without guilt. Still, I know God calls me to participate with him in caring for those marginalized and hurting neighbors of our world. And I want to learn how to respond.

Which is probably why the story of the woman with the issue of blood (found in Matt. 9:20–22, Mark 5:21–43, and Luke 8:43–48) has always grabbed my heart. In fact, I often think of Carol and that man whenever I read this Gospel story, probably because their interaction revealed to me the same Christlike boldness of what it means to touch publicly someone so seemingly untouchable. Who knows how long the man's dried blood had stayed caked across his forehead, why he was so exhausted and despondent, or what other ailments he'd suffered from as he wandered in from the streets? I just know that Carol's single silent act brought cleansing and dignity to this man, if only for a moment, just as it taught me a powerful lesson about unconditional service.

In the same way, the story of this "untouchable" nameless woman wandering the streets for twelve years, hunting for a cure from her wretched condition and searching for any semblance of relief, grips me. No physician could heal her. Though she'd spent all she had to get better, she only grew worse. (Even Luke, who was also a physician, admitted in chapter 8 verse 43 that doctors could not help her.) Nonetheless, when she heard that a popular young rabbi was passing through, she thought he might know how to help. Against cultural mores of the time, she pressed her weary body against the odds of a crowded street, hoping for even a brush against the man's robe. It was a desperate and bleak situation. But what happened next was also a striking reminder that the King of Kings came to earth to restore beauty, health, and dignity to those brave enough to come close when he passed by. And it is his presence still that provides the means to do just that.

Unlike the crippled woman in the synagogue whom Christ did touch, there is no record in the Gospels of his reaching out his hand and pressing it against this woman's forehead. Yet, we can be sure of this one thing: he *touched* a really tired, really sick woman on a really busy street while he was on his way somewhere else. Like the homeless man in Denver who knew enough to find reprieve at the coffeehouse, this woman, too, staggered into a crowded place, looking for any kind of help. Armed with a tiny bit of hope, this weary woman thought that maybe if she just touched the hem of the young rabbi's robe, something good might happen.

Immediately something did. And the exchange made all the difference.

## The Context

Many dynamics form the backdrop for this story in helping us better understand it. First, three of the four Gospel writers included the account of the "woman with the issue of blood," providing a full picture of the interaction between her and Jesus. Mark included the most details, perhaps because the apostle Peter had told him about his journeys with Jesus, and the two men were close confidants. (After all, Peter was beside Jesus that day, and Luke's Gospel named him as the disciple who questioned Jesus when the Lord asked who touched him in the crowd.) But all three writers clearly described this event as a story within a story.

The scene took place in Jesus's second year of ministry, referred to as his "year of popularity," just after he left the eastern region of the Sea of Galilee, where he'd been ministering to all kinds of people in all kinds of ways. He'd cast out demons, calmed storms, told stories, healed the sick, and attracted such crowds that his authority was growing as quickly as the animosity many religious leaders were feeling toward him. Still, no one could deny the impact his words and works were having on the people of the region.

Our nameless woman—known only for her issue of blood—felt that impact as did a synagogue ruler—a man whose name we *do* know. Jairus had heard that Christ's boat was docked nearby, so he hurried to Jesus and literally fell on his knees when he saw him. He begged the young rabbi to come heal his only daughter—whose name we also don't know. Obviously, Jairus had learned of Christ's work throughout the land, of the healings and miracles he'd performed, and couldn't help but plead for his twelve-year-old dying daughter.

He seemed like a good man, this Jairus. He was a father who cared for his little girl in a culture that didn't much value females, and a religious leader who wasn't afraid to publicly confess what he believed: that Jesus was able to heal. So he came and he asked, and Jesus did not say no. In fact, Mark recorded Christ's response to Jairus as simply, "So Jesus went with him." He did not pause and weigh the options, nor did he deliberate with his public relations team accompanying him about whether this would be a politically strategic use of his time. He made no comment like "Hmm, let me check my calendar" or "Let me pray about it first." He simply went with the man whose little girl was almost dead, who asked him to put his hands on her so that "she will be healed and live."

But with his growing popularity, going anywhere with Jesus was no easy task. A large crowd had gathered around him and pushed against him like fans around a star athlete in a baseball stadium. Shoulders pressed against hot shoulders on a dry, dusty road. Their pace was ridiculously unhurried—a blur of humanity in slow motion—because of the amount of people who'd come to see this hero. His disciples tried to do "crowd control," but that, too, was no easy job in those days.

Then another story broke into the strolling caravan of people en route to Jairus's home. A woman, a second-class citizen already, whose uterus had been hemorrhaging for *twelve years*—what contemporary woman can even imagine such trauma!—squeezed her way through the mass of men, religious leaders, and a few curious women. It was a gutsy move on her part since she was well aware of the stigma that hung over her head. The culture in which she lived officially prohibited rabbis from ever touching anyone who had been declared unclean. If they did, they would become ceremonially unclean themselves, and therefore unable to perform their pious duties. Since this woman was unquestionably unclean, she would surely contaminate any religious leader. In fact, lepers, and anyone similarly diseased (like her), were forced to live outside of the towns, far away from public places (like marketplaces or synagogues) so as not to spread their impurities, both physical and spiritual.

So for this woman even to be in the crowd was taboo. Because she'd been labeled an untouchable, an undesirable, she'd lived the last twelve years not only in enormous physical suffering but also on the fringe of a society that piously elevated holiness and purity as the ultimate way of life. She was weary on every level; poor from having spent all she had to get better, lonely from having no personal support system, and discouraged that she might never be able to live a normal life again. For over a decade she'd visited every type of unregulated doctor who performed God only knows what kind of "medical" experiments on her. When those didn't work, she went to every type of healer or spiritualist who fed her empty promises, and then on to every other quack or kook who tried to capitalize on her pain. She'd spent all she had and tried everything possible in hopes of getting better. Instead, she only grew worse.

The blood did not dry up. It never stopped flowing.

Any sense of control or power to function normally for this woman was depleted. Though she was obviously passionate about getting healed, no one could help. She was exhausted, disillusioned, alienated, and very, very sick. In fact, this woman became desperate almost to the point of irrationality, risking what was left of her life by staggering into a very public and frenzied place.

Though the cultural context might be different, the personal context in which this woman existed is not unlike that of many women I know today: ignored and relegated to the margins, overcome with feelings of ugliness, fear, and the inability to belong or contribute to society, and so tired from the effort of daily survival that nothing much matters.

But then someone told this woman about Jesus. About a man who'd loved other women like her and brought them back to life. Perhaps she figured she had nothing to lose, and so she made herself as invisible as possible by sneaking into the crowd when Jesus was on his way to heal someone else's daughter. She somehow concocted the plan that if she could just touch the hem of this guy's outer garment—the portion considered sacred—some relief might finally come to her. Regardless of the abuse she might take by entering such a public place, regardless of the possible rejection and disappointment she would once again endure, somehow she knew if she simply touched that edge, that tassel on the rabbi's robe, it might be enough. Then she could slip away just as she'd slipped into the crowd, and no one would be the wiser.

What she hadn't counted on, of course, was what the Lord did next.

## The Conflict

*Jesus is busy focusing on others, paying attention to the important people,* the woman probably thought as she inched her way forward. She was hoping no one would notice her, this insignificant sick woman who never wanted to bother the prophet nor detain him from his mission. All she wanted was a simple touch.

But the stakes were raised and getting higher all the time. On his way to care for an already dying girl, in the middle of a crowded street with many pressing needs and the suspicious eye of local leaders, Jesus no doubt felt the tension of the moment. Jairus was beside himself, worried for his only daughter. Peter and the other disciples were already concerned for their leader with the matters at hand. How much more when he suddenly stopped in the midst of the crowd, looked around, and asked the absurd question: "Who touched me?"

After having such a wretched illness for so long, this woman surely did not want any publicity. And considering the embarrassing ailment from which she suffered, Jesus could surely have left her alone. She was unclean, poor, and a public relations nightmare to an increasingly popular leader among the people. Everyone had already touched him in this crowd—everyone from sick or wealthy to young or crippled. No wonder Peter tried to reason with Jesus about his silly question. Who had time to stop and notice?

Jesus did. He always had time for those bold enough to seek him. Immediately, he knew that healing power had gone out of him—though not because this was some magical button that anyone could push and presto!—healing power would come forth. No, he knew faith was walking in the crowd, sneaking in and around the men walking beside him. He knew someone as desperate as Jairus for a touch of restoration was walking among them. And he was not embarrassed by her, no matter what condition she had or where she'd come from.

In spite of the odds against her, this woman had been nothing short of reckless, maybe even impulsive, about pursuing healing. But one confrontation with Jesus always leads to another deeper one. So he stopped in his tracks, looked around, asked the nuttiest question possible to those—like Peter—who weren't privy to his plans, and waited. He waited for the one who believed in him to come forward. To show herself.

Instead of turning around and sneaking home, this woman—who'd immediately felt the blood stop flowing in her when Christ's robe touched her—was terrified. She'd lived on the margins for years because of her condition and now was being asked to come center stage because she no longer had a condition! Though she had hidden herself because of her shame and defilement, now she was being asked to step into the limelight and confess she'd touched the rabbi. Would she be publicly rebuked for her indecent presence? Would she be ridiculed for her audacity? Would she be further marginalized and hauled away? She did not know; she only knew the master had asked a question, and she knew the answer, one that made her tremble in fear.

As she fell on her knees in front of Jesus, Jairus, and Peter and the rest of them staring in panicked dismay, she could not contain herself. She rambled on and on about how and why she'd suffered for so long, how and why she'd come that day. And she waited for her punishment for having violated Jewish law, for having potentially contaminated the crowd as well as the religious leaders. She waited for the wrath of God to descend on her.

She received grace instead. Christ did not call her forward to embarrass her, to condemn her, or even to add to the increasing anxiety Jairus and the others must have been feeling by now as she staggered forward and dropped to her knees. He brought her forward because she was *not* insignificant to him—no one ever is—nor was she bothering him in the least. Jesus already knew she'd been healed, but he wanted to hold her up as an example of faith, of one who, though she lacked any sense of self-worth, did not allow it to paralyze her belief and acknowledgment of who he was and what he could do. In her, he could show the splendor of his powerful touch, the might of his restoration and healing. And he was in no hurry to do otherwise.

As she waited for judgment, she received another glorious display of grace. Just as she had before been publicly condemned as an untouchable, now in the presence of everyone, Jesus declared her free from her ailment and therefore no longer marginalized. If she had merely gone home, few might have known her condition had improved; now he was giving her his stamp of affirmation and including her in his community. He was showing his affection for her by looking her in the eye and touching her with his words, words that all the world could hear (and still hears): "Daughter, your faith has healed you. Go in peace and be freed from your suffering."

**The Counsel**

Obviously, we can learn much from her story about the power of touch, about the role of bold faith in the midst of dismal circumstances, and about the unexpected ways God rewards those who seek him. All these are true lessons to glean from this story within a story, but I think there is something else that is crucial to understand from the short yet profound interaction between the woman with the issue of blood and Jesus of Nazareth. In fact, I think it is a lesson that has implications beyond the healing elements of this real-life example.

That is simply this: Christ must have known that her public confession was not just about her healing. Though of course it was a very personal intervention as it freed her from the nightmare of an illness that had consumed her life. But her public proclamation must have been amazing for others as well. It must have, for instance, encouraged

Jairus that he had asked the *right* rabbi after all to come and heal his daughter. It must have reassured Peter and the other disciples who had given up all to follow this man and wander the streets of the cities with him. And certainly, it must have had an incredible impact on those who'd known this woman, on those who knew how many kooks and methods and doctors she'd tried just to get better. No longer would they have to wonder and cry aloud with her, "How long, oh Lord, how long?"

In other words, just as our choices—good or bad—never merely affect us personally but always have a ripple effect on the people with whom we come in contact, so, too, does the work of God in our lives influence those around us. This woman who'd spent twelve years dying from a hemorrhage of blood and steering clear of people now had been proclaimed clean for all to see. God's gift was—and is—a visible reminder that he is interested in restoring the lives of those who have been broken, battered, and desperate. He has always welcomed into his community of friends those who have been alienated by fear and relegated to the fringe of society. Just as Jesus cared deeply for this woman's well-being, so was she—and all of us like her—the very reason behind his mission.

We know too that Jesus went on in this story not to *heal* Jairus's little girl but to bring her back to life! Perhaps Jairus had been emboldened by the woman's faith and Christ's response to it. I can't help but think that is so. And because Jesus knew this woman had been passionate about pursuing her healing, he must have known she would come forward when he called. He knew this was an opportunity to use her boldness in declaring his works, works that everyone needed to see!

We still do. Yes, her public declaration of his touch signaled how she no longer would live in the bondage of her sickness, fear, and alienation. Nor would people assume Jesus had some magical power to heal if only they touched him. No, Christ called her forward to show the direct relationship between her faith and the release of God's power. Though there might have been a primitive superstition about touching a rabbi's robe, Jesus clarified that divine power often responds to human faith. What she wanted to do secretly because of the shame of her illness, he turned to good so all could see the power of his touch. Then he blessed her with God's peace, and by bringing her before him, their personal relationship was secured.

Her healing was not merely physical—it was relational, spiritual, emotional, and cultural. Finally, she was clean. Finally, she was restored. Finally, she was honored as a healthy woman in the presence of all who'd avoided her on the street.

Consequently, I believe he asks us to be equally bold in our declaration of his work in our lives—whether we're relieved of our suffering through his grace or asked to endure it with him. When we point others to him in spite of our circumstances, it is not only for our sake but for theirs. Is that easy? No, she knelt there trembling. But now that she was whole, she was free to take risks in living well rather than staying stuck in an illness that could keep her self-absorbed. We are too. Just as her immense shame was overcome in one word—*Daughter*—so, too, does he establish a relationship, connection, and identity with us for others to see. Not to embarrass us but to point others to his splendor.

How could he call her daughter? How could he ask her, or any of us, to publicly step forward for his sake, or to touch those whom our world might otherwise call untouchable? Because he knew that soon enough he would be taking on the suffering of humankind when he chose to go to the cross. He knew that he would bleed for us in order to stop the hemorrhaging of human illnesses, spiritual and physical. He knew that his public sacrifice would become our personal freedom, his pain would bring us peace.

### The Conversion

It was Christ's work and his words that delivered this woman from a lifetime of desperate suffering. She did not get well *before* she found her way into the crowd; she did so only when she encountered the power of the living God made flesh, the One who dwelled among us. And that is still the way we are empowered to receive his gifts of healing, salvation, and bold faith: through *his* work and *his* words within us.

The pressure is off.

After all, what did Jesus say to this woman that reflected her conversion, the change in her life? He said, "Daughter, your faith has healed you. Go in *peace*." What was that faith? Her relentless and single-minded focus on *him*! That was her point of conversion, when she moved from fear of dying to the relief of living, from daily despair to endless joy, from social alienation and defilement to personal connection and purity. And mostly from constant anxiety to lasting peace. His peace. Yes, a woman of pain and ugliness quite literally became a woman of new strength and beauty.

And he invites us to the same adventure, to sneak into the crowd where he might be passing through and brush up against him. For some of us, that might mean collapsing in a chair, a cut across our forehead, and allowing his fingers to cleanse us. It might mean stepping forward and proclaiming that the pain somehow stopped, that he took it away and we're free to be who he's always wanted us to be. For others it might mean trusting him enough to endure what's thrown into our bodies, so we may experience the privilege of suffering *with* him. No doubt it will look different for each of us, but each will display his splendor. And he will touch us in powerful, unexpected ways when we pursue him in faith.

For beauty and wholeness come only through the touch of the One who created us, the One whose death gives us life, who became poor so we might become rich, whose suffering means that not only does he know our pain, but he also desires our healing. It is that life of fellowship *with* him that he lived and died for. As the poet-prophet Isaiah wrote, "He took up our infirmities and carried our sorrows, yet we considered him stricken by God, smitten by him, and afflicted. But he was pierced for our transgressions, he was crushed for our iniquities; the punishment that brought us peace was upon him, and by his wounds we are healed" (Isa. 53:4–5).

# In-Between Reflection

1. Have you ever had a friend like Carol? How did she set an example for you?

2. How has your body and health served you throughout your life?

3. For twelve years, this woman pursued treatments to cure her terrible condition. She was desperate and believed if she just touched Christ's garment, she would be healed. What part of her story most connects with you?

4. How do you think the woman might have felt when Jesus said, "Who touched me?" How do you think she felt when he called her "Daughter"?

5. What new insights about Jesus does this story inspire for you?

6. Can you remember a time when it was difficult for you to publicly confess God's grace? What happened?

7. Perhaps there are some areas in your life you've felt have "held you hostage," or over which you've experienced either physical or emotional pain. If you feel comfortable, ask some Christian friends to pray for you, that you may know the power of Christ's presence and touch. And consider praying the same for others, asking God to increase your faith.

## DIGGING DEEPER

No human has ever been exempt from the trials of health challenges, sicknesses, or weariness. Our contemporary culture seems obsessed with diet fads, medical research, and cultivating "healthy habits" in an attempt to sidestep physical suffering. Certainly, many of these are gifts of God's provision for helping us live well. But suffering—according to Scripture—does not have to keep us from enjoying God's presence. It can be redemptive. Examine the following verses in light of the story of the woman with the issue of blood: Job 35:15, Luke 24:26, and 1 Peter 4:1–12. What role does suffering play in each, and what does it suggest to those of us living in a culture addicted to comfortableness?

What other biblical stories help you better understand suffering and God's sovereign purposes?

# PREPARATION

### Jesus Raises a Widow's Son

[11]Soon afterward, Jesus went to a town called Nain, and his disciples and a large crowd went along with him. [12]As he approached the town gate, a dead person was being carried out—the only son of his mother, and she was a widow. And a large crowd from the town was with her. [13]When the Lord saw her, his heart went out to her and he said, "Don't cry."

[14]Then he went up and touched the coffin, and those carrying it stood still. He said, "Young man, I say to you, get up!" [15]The dead man sat up and began to talk, and Jesus gave him back to his mother.

[16]They were all filled with awe and praised God. "A great prophet has appeared among us," they said. "God has come to help his people." [17]This news about Jesus spread throughout Judea and the surrounding country.

When you are ready, continue reflecting on the following question:

Perhaps you've read this story before. What new insights or observations jumped out to you as you read her story anew in this Gospel account? Jot them down. Take a few moments to reflect before reading chapter 5.

**Prayer:** *What an astonishing thing it is, O Giver of Life, that you would enter our grief to renew our hope! Thank you. Amen.*

Desperate Women of the Bible

---

5

---

# DEAD WOMAN WALKING

I thought I would never take in a full, easy breath again.
I'd wake up and the first light on my face and the first air
in my lungs would shoot me full of that heavy pain. I'd fall
back into bed and just try not to be. But I kept being.

Vinita Hampton Wright, *Velma Still Cooks in Leeway*

In the 1950s, a middle-aged college professor fell in love for
probably the first time in his life. For years he had contented
himself with his teaching and his writing. He'd filled his
days with scholarly efforts, class lectures, and constant
research. Apart from his regular attendance at the church
down the road, the only social life he had was at a local café
where he'd join colleagues each week for animated discus-
sions on literature, poetry, and stories. Year after year, the
habits of his life—church, reading, teaching, writing, and
intellectual conversations—became so engrained that he
did not think he needed anything, or anyone, else.

---

Until one day when he received a curious letter from a woman. She had read some of his writings and wanted to respond to the author directly. He wrote her back as was his custom when people sent him letters about his work. And for the next two years, she'd reply to his letters and he'd do the same each time he received one from her.

Before either knew it, they were forging an intriguing friendship, one whose depths neither had before experienced. They'd write to each other about theology, art, politics, or themselves, risking a little more of their feelings and their insights with each new letter. Eventually, the woman took a brave step: she wrote to tell the professor she would be traveling from her country to his to pay him a visit. She wanted to meet the writer who'd so influenced her thinking, to talk face to face with the fifty-four-year-old single professor with whom she'd been corresponding so frequently.

They arranged to meet for tea in the lobby of a local hotel near the college where the professor taught. Before her, the only romance he'd really known was what he'd read in books or observed from friends. But here was a woman whose intellect matched his, whose wit challenged him, and whose new Christian faith inspired him. She captivated him in ways no one else ever had—though he wasn't about to admit it.

Not long after they'd met, she moved to his country, and her friendship became such a valuable part of his life, growing into a deeper relationship, that he quietly knew he wanted more. Yes, she'd been married before, and he did not believe in divorce. But, he wrestled with himself, her husband had been unfaithful, and she had tried to be a good wife and mother to her two sons.

The more time they spent together, the more the professor fell for the woman—so much so that he married her twice! The first time they exchanged vows they went secretly (to protect his reputation) to a civil government office in 1956. Years later some claimed they married then simply so she could obtain proper citizenship in her new country. Others believed she loved him, and he was simply doing her a favor. But why would a man as principled and intellectually rigorous as he—though probably out of touch with his emotions at the time—have acted so flippantly? No matter what the skeptics said, I believe the professor sincerely cared for this woman.

In her, he'd literally and figuratively met his match.

But then the unthinkable happened. Only six months after their "wedding" she was diagnosed with the same disease that had killed his mother when he was only nine years old and his father when he was a young man: cancer. It zapped her strength and reduced a once-vigorous woman to resting her days away in a hospital bed. Watching her quick deterioration, the man who'd lived most of his life in his academic head suddenly had more feelings than he knew what to do with. He agonized over his wife's condition and lamented the loss of her health. He grieved for the pain she experienced while at the same time grew more deeply appreciative of her friendship. His love deepened. He knew it, and this time he wasn't afraid to admit it.

That's when he did the only right thing he could think to do: he married her again. This time a clergyman from their church officiated the wedding—at her bedside in the hospital. Publicly. And in what was surely a miracle, God gave her body a reprieve from the cancer for the next few years. They traveled to Ireland and Greece. She moved her sons into his home. They laughed and they walked and they prayed. He continued to read, to write, and to teach, and she continued to challenge him with her words, her writing, and her wit. It was a most unexpected and unusual marriage.

But the cancer came back. Exactly ten years after he'd received his first letter from her, the professor's wife—with him by her side—gave way to death. A few days later, he buried her, and a few weeks and months later, he cried out to God. Why had God allowed his wife to die? Where was God's kindness in that? What possible good would her loss serve?

His questions took him eventually—as they always had—to prayer and to writing. And a year after her death, the professor published one of the most personal and important books he'd written in his long literary career. This book was about his wife's life and death, about his feelings of loss and pain, and he called it simply *A Grief Observed*. It was so personal in fact that he published it under another name, the pseudonym of N. W. Clerk.

Three years later on the same November day in 1963 that President John F. Kennedy died, the professor known as Clive Staples Lewis died of a heart attack at the home he'd shared with his wife, Joy Davidman Gresham, her two sons, and his brother. Had he lived just one more week Lewis would have turned sixty-five years old. And though his books were enormously popular and influential during his lifetime, works by the Oxford don have become better known since his death. From his Ransom Trilogy and the Chronicles of Narnia to his classics in Christian apologetics (*Mere Christianity, The Screwtape Letters*, etc.) and literary criticism, Lewis's influence as one of the previous century's most astute Christian thinkers and writers has been far reaching. Who among believers and skeptics alike today has not been affected in some way by his works?

But it is the real love story that "Jack" and Joy shared that has profoundly moved many, many people, inspiring four plays, a major feature film (*Shadowlands*), and countless writings. Perhaps because it severely tested the faith of such a great Christian thinker, revealing a seemingly "normal" side to the otherwise brilliant professor. His love for Joy had been great, surprising even, and therefore the depths of his sorrow must have felt even greater. In some ways, her death became the most difficult teacher he had ever had. As one critic wrote, "C. S. Lewis joined the human race when his wife, Joy Gresham, died of cancer. Lewis, the Oxford don whose Christian apologetics make it seem like he's got an answer for everything, experienced crushing doubt for the first time after his wife's tragic death."[1]

Losing Joy sent Lewis spiraling into an emotion he'd avoided most of his life: grief. He became like a dead man walking. He grew despondent, questioned his friends and his faith, and wandered through the habits of his teaching life with bland indifference. "Her absence is like the sky, spread over everything," he wrote in his book. He went on to describe how her face was becoming blurred in his memory, while her voice was still vivid. "The remembered voice—that can turn me at any moment to a whimpering child."

Yet, the whimpering child also grew into a man of deeper faith, recognizing somehow that there was much to gain from such despair, making more real his belief in the Almighty. "Your bid—for God or no God, for a good God or the Cosmic Sadist, for eternal life or non-entity—will not be serious if nothing much is staked on it. And you will never discover how serious it was until the stakes are raised horribly high," he wrote. "God has not been trying an experiment on my faith or love in order to find out their quality. He knew it already. It was I who didn't."[2]

The grief that Lewis confronted when he lost the wife he never thought he'd have must have been excruciating—as anyone who has ever lost a loved one knows. Your entire body becomes a storm of conflicting emotions, and your faith in anything is challenged and often found wanting. Doubt seems normal. Hope seems far away. Death covers everything you hear and see and touch. It is as Lewis described, "Nothing will shake a man—or at any rate a man like me—out of his merely verbal thinking and his merely notional beliefs. He has to be knocked silly before he comes to his senses. Only torture will bring out the truth. Only under torture does he discover it himself."[3]

## A Woman of Grief

In the last years of his life, C. S. Lewis became a man who lived daily with enormous grief. His wife's death was perhaps one of the most painful losses he'd ever encountered, and yet remarkably—and very publicly—it eventually drew him closer to the One who'd first introduced him to Joy. Gradually, that grief reinforced the faith behind his life's works and drove him deeper into prayer, encouraging in the process thousands of readers in similar situations to do the same. In fact, the last manuscript he prepared for publication before his death was a book on prayer called *Letters to Malcolm: Chiefly on Prayer.*

If Lewis's response to Joy's death shows us anything, it is that grief is an overwhelming human and genderless emotion. Men and women alike of all ages and cultures experience its ravaging effects on their souls, and I can't help but think that the Creator of the universe is moved to sorrow as well each time someone grieves over the death of a loved one. Thankfully, Lewis wrote about his grief in a way that points anyone who reads his work back to the God of comfort. But Lewis first discovered this God from another book that has influenced more people than any other by any single writer.

The whole of Scripture communicates the journey of life and death, joy and grief, pain and hope that comprises the human condition. Over and over, it tells the story of God's intervention in the lives of real men and women, those weak mortal creatures who encountered great sorrow and despair in the daily tasks of living and were in desperate need of a power greater than their own just to get them to tomorrow. Yet each story reminds us that God—not death—has the final say.

The Gospel writers told the inspired truths of the griefs they observed or heard about. From Matthew, Mark, Luke, and John, we know that Christ responded often to the intense emotions he encountered in hurting people, just as we know of his culturally radical interactions with a variety of wounded but passionate women, meeting each need in a unique way. To a thirsty and promiscuous woman, he gave true satisfaction and a new purpose. To a crippled and alienated woman he gave healing and belonging. To a poor but generous widow he gave honor and esteem, and to a woman plagued with an issue of blood, he gave restoration and dignity.

Perhaps more astounding still is the story we come to now in Luke 7:11–17, the story of Christ's seemingly accidental encounter with a grieving woman. It is an unbearably sad tale: a woman who had already lost her husband was now burying her only son. There was sorrow upon sorrow for this woman; anger, loneliness, and despair must have filled every cell in her body. As she staggered beside the corpse of her son, his lifeless body stretched out in an open coffin, she knew she had nothing left to believe. Hope had been stolen from her, and there was no reason to keep going. She was simply a walking *dead* woman.

When Jesus "happened" upon the funeral procession at the edge of the small town called Nain, he could not help but observe the grieving woman. Luke wrote, in fact, that when the Lord saw her, "his heart went out to her." This phrase "heart went out" used the Greek word for compassion (which means "to suffer with"), and it is not difficult to imagine why seeing her would have been upsetting to Jesus. To watch a mother wailing over the death of her child, to know she was on her way to drop him in a grave after she had already buried his father, would have been traumatic for any human with even a tinge of conscience in him, let alone God in the flesh. It was a miserable scenario for every person present—but especially for the One who knew life was not supposed to be like this.

His response was completely spontaneous, for Jesus apparently was not familiar with this woman or her son. He had not been informed of the funeral. No one had read him the boy's obituary in the *Nain Daily News,* and he'd never gotten a call from the woman's distant cousin asking him to come to the funeral and lend his moral support. Yet, once he stopped on the road and watched the procession, his *heart went out* to the woman. He could not bear to witness the utter darkness that came when a mother buried her child, when a human being had to surrender a loved one because of the cruelty of mortal laws.

Compassion, however, was the blood in Christ's veins. It moved him to respond to suffering in ways no human had ever known but had always yearned to experience. He was not intimidated by death—he was moved by it. And his presence was going to make all the difference for a widow who never could have imagined what was about to happen.

### The Context

Jesus had been traveling already throughout this region, calling people to a life of faith in him, preaching to the crowds, and healing the sick. When he arrived at Nain, he was about thirty-one years old and already into the second year of his ministry. Nain was not far from the village where his feet would be washed with the tears of a sinful woman (but that is our next chapter).

We already know that the writer-doctor known as Luke was deeply concerned with the social issues of the time, and consequently his Gospel highly honored women. Christ's encounter at Nain, in fact, was only recorded in Luke's Gospel, and considering the status of women at that time, let alone the status of widows, it was no small thing that Luke included it at all. Commentators consider this story one of the most striking incidents of Christ's life on earth, perhaps because it was the first time Luke referred to him as "the Lord." But it was certainly a fitting title considering Jesus displayed incredible human compassion while responding with supernatural power, exercising his power over death.

The scene took place as Christ, his disciples, and the large crowd who'd surrounded him approached the town. As they did, they could not help but stop still when they reached the gates. A funeral procession was passing, and Jewish custom expected the crowd to respond in reverence. A silence must have come over them, making the weeping of the procession all the more wrenching. Jewish tradition required that its people perform regular works of love, and attending a funeral ranked among one of the higher works. Mourning the death of an only son was all the greater, and Jesus would have known all about these customs.

Jewish law also required that a body be buried as soon as possible after death for both religious and health reasons. There was no embalming in those days, so apart from the spices and ointments often used to prepare a person for burial, the stench of death could begin to rise within a day or so. Which was perhaps why burials took place outside of the city. And because a corpse was considered ceremonially unclean and impure, it was off limits to rabbis and religious leaders. Only "unholy" men were allowed to carry it.

Luke did not provide any details about who this woman was, how her son died, or how recently she'd become a widow. We only know that as she was about to bury her only son, she was not even conscious Jesus was there. There was no indication that she even knew who he was nor that she expected anything from him. Instead, because her boy was now gone, she must have been caught up with the feelings of immense loss and worry about who would provide for her from here on. Her husband—the sole provider in this male-dominated culture—had already died and left her to try to mete out an existence. Now without the additional help her son might have provided, she could be left to beg or borrow, to depend on the kindness of others merely to make it from day to day.

Perhaps her grief was for her future as well as the loss of her loved one. And perhaps Jesus was responding to this as well.

## The Conflict

However bleak the widow's future must have seemed to her, it could not have appeared much worse than the present pain that overwhelmed her. She was beyond desperate. She would never again hear her boy laugh or watch him play or admire how he'd grown. He had already breathed his last breath, his funeral was already taking place, and she had nothing more for which to live. Even the memories ached.

It was a scene of enormous tension, and to the human eye the stakes could not have been higher. What else could anyone do? The ultimate foe had already ended a significant chapter for the woman and her friends. Death had won and in doing so had reminded the people surrounding the corpse that the precedent had been set for them as well. Someday they, too, would meet this fate. No one could make this reality, or the dread that accompanied it, go away. What else could anyone do except grieve with the widow and cry out to God? What could a young rabbi from another town possibly offer except his condolences and respect as he and his friends passed through?

But this was no ordinary man who crashed this funeral. When he saw the woman, his heart broke for her. Yet, when it did, he said a most unusual thing to her. He walked right next to her, looked her in the eye, and whispered, "Don't cry."

Don't cry?! This woman was a widow, her son was dead, and she was in the process of burying him. How could she hold back her tears? Why should she? How could she respond any other way to death than to grieve and mourn that it had stolen her two loved ones from her life? But Jesus hadn't told the widow *not* to grieve, as if grief were not important. Nor did he simply patronize her by patting her hand and saying, "There, there. It'll be all right." Why, then, did he say "Don't cry"? Either his comment was ridiculously insensitive and mean, implying she just needed to pull it together and move on, or he knew something she did not. He knew something beyond tears was about to happen.

Yes, his word was as good as his deed. His action and his comment could not be separated. Luke wrote that Jesus was moved to compassion, which meant that he genuinely felt for this mother as she cried; yet he also knew death was not as final as it seemed. He could say this to her because he was anticipating that something else was about to take place.

Something did. What happened next must have really disturbed the people, since they all knew what religious law said about rabbis and corpses. As Jesus approached the coffin where the dead man lay, he did two things no one had seen before. The men carrying the coffin froze as they watched the young rabbi first contaminate himself with the impurities of the dead body by touching the coffin. But then their eyes grew even wider.

As if to say, "Oh no, you don't!" Jesus then took death on. He reached out his hand, held the corpse's fingers in his, and told the young man to get up. The boy then *sat up* in front of all of them—very much alive—and started talking! Jesus helped him down from the coffin and presented him back to his mother, who if she had not fainted from astonishment was weeping not from grief but from the extraordinary fact that her child was breathing in her arms! Again!

## The Counsel

What a wonder! Who today could imagine visiting a funeral home, passing the open casket, and having the corpse suddenly sit up and chat as if nothing had ever happened? A bizarre event like this is difficult for the modern mind to imagine. But to the people in Christ's day, raising the dead to life was one of the signs they'd been expecting of a Messiah who would usher in his kingdom. The encounter at Nain must have reminded the crowd of the prophet Elijah and the widow in 1 Kings 17, when Elijah pleaded for the breath to be returned to the widow's son. And in fact, Nain was near the same place where God answered Elijah's prayer and created the expectation in his people for a future king to do likewise.

The widow, disciples, and crowd around Jesus had witnessed a great miracle when they saw life return to the dead boy. They were filled with awe and praise—who wouldn't be?—and believed God had sent them another Elijah. They believed that God himself had visited them. But they—like all humans—were not necessarily sure *this* rabbi could be their Savior. Yes, they'd just witnessed an extraordinary miracle, one they'd never seen before, which stunned them and made them marvel.

Tomorrow, however—mere mortals that they were—they might forget.

Nonetheless, as Eugene Peterson described the scene in his New Testament translation known as *The Message*, Nain that day was "a place of holy mystery." God *was* at work when Christ's compassionate action restored the life of a young man and kept a family together. What the people did not know was that this man who'd just told the boy to get up—and would do the same with his friend Lazarus and Jairus's daughter—would also go on to make the claim that he actually *was* the resurrection.

Nothing, not even death, was too difficult for him.

Through absolutely no good deed or profession of faith on the widow's part, he extended comfort when it seemed absurd. He offered life when only death seemed certain. He gave back the only child to a widow and in the process resurrected her hope for the future.

Though the people that day could not have known what was in store for the young rabbi, Jesus did. He knew that he would face death for their sake. He would grieve the excruciating loss of his friends and his Father, but he would be able to endure it because he knew that was not all there was. He knew death was not unbeatable. His life, ministry, and death all pointed to the truth and reality of this one thing: resurrection.

His entire purpose was to make all things new. His time on earth was to restore us to heaven, to provide new life through his death as the *only Son* of God.

The miracle at Nain signaled another miracle to come, one where he would die so we could live, where his claim as the resurrection hope would become the anchor for anyone in life who had known—or would know—unbearable grief. He would take our place on the cross so that we might not fear death but instead know the Author of life.

His temporary absence would become our eternal Presence.

This fact of history is what sets Christianity apart from all other religions or belief systems. After his death on the cross the risen Lord appeared first to women (John 20), then to his ragtag disciples, and finally to over five hundred people (1 Cor. 15:6). A spectacular mystery indeed! And unless many people were hallucinating that afternoon, the unprecedented reality of Christ's resurrection became the foundation upon which the church was built for believers throughout the ages.

It is one that certainly offers the same foundation for our precarious lives today, because unlike any other religion, the center of our faith is not decomposing in a grave.

He is alive. And he is still moved to compassion.

## The Conversion

As a result of Christ's miracle at Nain, many people believed in the Lord (Luke 7:16–17). The news of the young man's resurrection spread throughout the surrounding country and inspired many who before had known only despair. Even the disciple Peter, who'd watched Jesus perform that mighty deed, was affected. Luke went on to write in Acts 9:36–43 that Peter himself prayed over a dead widow named Tabitha and she, too, was brought back to life!

The widow of Nain moved Jesus to great compassion. When he responded, she and her son were quite literally changed, taken from death and grief to the marvel of new life and hope. A woman of despair became a woman whose lifeless soul had been revived, a woman who dramatically experienced the joy of reconciliation and the power of restoration. She was not changed by following a ten-step plan to overcome her grief but by a living, breathing Story. By the reality of the hope Christ, the risen Lord, offered when he came to her, as he comes to us, to those who are *desperate*.

Jesus not only changed the widow's circumstance by bringing back her son but also communicated to her and everyone who heard the news that death would no longer have the final say. Resurrection was possible *with him*. And if it were possible at Nain, it would be possible again. This life was not all there was.

Now the widow had a reason to keep walking.

Even two thousand years after her story, we know how real her situation was. We live in a world where the daily news reflects the awful grief of mothers losing their sons and daughters to war, children watching their parents killed in hurricanes, husbands losing their wives to cancer. Tragedy parades its cruel images across our television screens each night and often steps into our own lives as well. We don't know what might happen when we walk out our door in the morning or if we will return that night. And because of this, many people fulfill what Hebrews 2:15 has claimed for centuries: they live their whole lives enslaved to the fear of death. (Producers even tease this out in a TV show called *Fear Factor*, as if life itself is not full enough of frightening episodes!)

But certainly Someone who has conquered death is worthy of belief—even in the midst of despair. One who entered the broken relationships of earth and lived out the promise of a wholeness to come is worth trusting right now. Every day the stakes are as high as they can get for us as humans because death and sin wait to devour us, our families, or our friends on every corner. The Good News, though, is that Jesus Christ confirmed the fact that a much better life awaits us. *That* is the Hope Factor on which we can place our lives.

It's been said that as long as prisoners of war had something to look forward to, they could endure any trauma of their confinement. Strip a prisoner of his hope, and he would resign himself to death. But if he knew his family or loved ones were waiting for him at home, he could survive the daily grief inflicted on him.

For us who believe in the home Christ has prepared, the place where we will eternally celebrate his life and presence in the family he has brought together from all the nations, nothing on this planet can steal our hope. As long as our hearts look forward to the reality that he waits for us and invites us to the beautiful fellowship of the holy Trinity, no affliction will ever be unbearable. In the process, his compassion *toward* us creates daily compassion *in* us to offer to others.

How do we know? Because the grave could not contain him! Scripture confirmed how Christ's resurrection pointed to the hope of eternal life. And those of us who cling to its place in history two thousand years ago as well as our future home are in good company with millions of people from all cultures and times who have also believed. Scores of thoughtful, gifted, and creative people through the ages have acknowledged this seemingly irrational, science-defying event as *the* single truth on which the Christian faith is centered.

Yes, the story of Christ's death and resurrection sustains us and encourages us to remember that we are not made merely for this life but for the one to come. We are created for another place. Our story is part of a bigger story.

As Lewis himself wrote, "If I find in myself a desire which no experience in this world can satisfy, the most probable explanation is that I was made for another world."[4]

This is *not* all there is!

# In-Between Reflection

1. In what ways has C. S. Lewis influenced your thinking? If his personal story is new to you, how did it affect you? (You might consider renting the film *Shadowlands* to review Lewis's life anew, or read some of his writings.)

2. The Scripture says Jesus's heart went out to *this* woman (a widow, probably poor, grieving for her only son) and so reflects his passion for the marginalized. How does this affect your perspective of the Lord and how he wants you to respond to those who are suffering?

3. Why do you think Jesus "went up and *touched* the coffin"?

4. Consider a time you lost someone to death. How does the story of the widow of Nain speak to you in regard to your loss?

5. What does this passage communicate to you about hope and the reality of the resurrection? Does it change or affect your view of grief and of death?

6. How does the miracle of new life affect the community of people in Nain? What are its implications for your life and community?

## Digging Deeper

All of us will know the grief and pain of losing a loved one at some point in our lives. Personal loss can take its emotional, spiritual, and even physical toll on us. Yet the Bible confirms over and over again God's commitment to his people in providing hope in the midst of loss, joy after times of mourning. Examine the following verses in light of the story of the widow of Nain: 1 Kings 17, 2 Kings 4, and 2 Corinthians 1:2–11. What role does the hope of the gospel play in your community as you reach out to others?

What impact does the resurrection of Jesus Christ have on you, the culture in which you live, and the friends/colleagues with whom you are in relationships?

# Preparation

## Jesus Anointed by a Sinful Woman

[36]Now one of the Pharisees invited Jesus to have dinner with him, so he went to the Pharisee's house and reclined at the table. [37]When a woman who had lived a sinful life in that town learned that Jesus was eating at the Pharisee's house, she brought an alabaster jar of perfume, [38]and as she stood behind him at his feet weeping, she began to wet his feet with her tears. Then she wiped them with her hair, kissed them and poured perfume on them.

[39]When the Pharisee who had invited him saw this, he said to himself, "If this man were a prophet, he would know who is touching him and what kind of woman she is—that she is a sinner."

[40]Jesus answered him, "Simon, I have something to tell you."

"Tell me, teacher," he said.

[41]"Two men owed money to a certain moneylender. One owed him five hundred denarii, and the other fifty. [42]Neither of them had the money to pay him back, so he canceled the debts of both. Now which of them will love him more?"

[43]Simon replied, "I suppose the one who had the bigger debt canceled."

"You have judged correctly," Jesus said.

[44]Then he turned toward the woman and said to Simon, "Do you see this woman? I came into your house. You did not give me any water for my feet, but she wet my feet with her tears and wiped them with her hair. [45]You did not give me a kiss, but this woman, from the time I entered, has not stopped kissing my feet. [46]You did not put oil on my head, but she has poured perfume on my feet. [47]Therefore, I tell

you, her many sins have been forgiven—for she loved much. But he who has been forgiven little loves little."

⁴⁸Then Jesus said to her, "Your sins are forgiven."

⁴⁹The other guests began to say among themselves, "Who is this who even forgives sins?"

⁵⁰Jesus said to the woman, "Your faith has saved you; go in peace."

When you are ready, continue reflecting on the following question:

Perhaps you've read this story before. What new insights or observations jumped out to you as you read her story anew in this Gospel account? Jot them down. Take a few moments to reflect before reading chapter 6.

**Prayer:** *"Father, you are full of compassion, I commit and commend myself unto you, in whom I am, and live, and know. Be the Goal of my pilgrimage, and my Rest by the way. Let my soul take refuge from the crowding turmoil of worldly thoughts beneath the shadow of your wings; let my heart, this sea of restless waves, find peace in you, O God. Amen."*

St. Augustine (African church father),
*Little Book of Prayers*

## 6

# CRY ME A RIVER

I could feel the tears brimming and sloshing in me like water in a glass that is unsteady and too full.

Sylvia Plath, *The Bell Jar*

It is no accident that humans have been given the gift of imagination. Because of our abilities to imagine, we can re-call the first time we rode a bicycle or felt our grandmother's wrinkled fingers or tasted the salty ocean on our lips. We can even "visit" the future as we prepare for a long-awaited reunion or find the courage to pack up our lives and move to another city. We see ourselves there, listening to new or old sounds, turning off the lights at night before heading to bed. Remembering life's events or imagining those still to come connects us to each moment, each transition, and each exchange, enriching our perspectives and invigorating our gratitude in the process.

The same can be said of the Christian journey. When we bring our imagination to the Scriptures, we can't help but travel across time and feel the sandy roads on which Jesus himself walked. We hear the winds on the Sea of Galilee and see the fishermen, tax collectors, and beggars crowd around the popular young rabbi from Nazareth. And when we watch in our mind's eye the red blood splattered from the whips across his back, we cannot help but grasp a little more clearly the depth and width and breadth of his love for us.

Yes, the gift of imagination anchors our hope and deepens our trust. As Eugene Peterson wrote, "Ages of faith have always been ages rich in imagination. It is easy to see why: the materiality of the Gospel (the seen, heard, and touched Jesus) is no less impressive than its spirituality (faith, hope, and love). Imagination is the mental tool we have for connecting material and spiritual, visible and invisible, earth and heaven."[1]

So when we imagine the real, breathing, and aching women and men who interacted with the Lord every time he came near, we *connect* a little more deeply with his goodness and grace. Earth and heaven intersect again. We hear his soft voice as he talks with those others ignore, watch him as he soothes and ministers to those others haven't even noticed, and we marvel, especially when we see him challenge the local leaders by defending a most questionable woman . . .

### A Woman of Tears (and The *Smell of Dignity*)

The early morning sun sliced the sky, stinging the woman's eyes as she stumbled down the road. It had been a difficult night for her, more so than usual, and her head pounded from a terrible ache. She stopped to lean against a wall when the sun smacked her face; then she covered her eyes with throbbing hands and wished she could shut them for a long time. She wanted to sleep without being bothered, to rest without being harassed.

She rubbed her neck slowly, pressing her thumbs deep into the muscle to work out her pain. Relief escaped from her lungs, and she started walking again, slowly, deliberately, just to get to the small room she rented away from the district where she did her work. She remembered the small coin purse strapped to her waist and ran her hand across it as if to protect it. And within a few minutes, the sun fell full across the road, making her blink and look away.

A brawny man suddenly bumped into her on the road, grumbling something to her about business and then grabbing the ends of her hair as it bounced off her shoulders. She jumped out of his reach and quickened her pace. Her eyes burned. And for just a moment, she thought of the day when she might leave this place. Maybe someday she would have enough money to get to the next town, where she could start over again. Anything would be better—had to be better—than this. But the thought was a cruel tease—nothing ever changed—so she hurried on.

It was dark in her room as she pushed the door closed and stepped toward the table. She reached for a small bowl, opened its lid, dropped the coins from her purse in it, and set the bowl back in its place. Then she undressed and splashed some water across her face before lying down to rest her bones. She exhaled a gentle sigh, though nothing in her being felt relaxed. In fact, it usually took her a long time to calm herself after a night of drunken customers. Still, she was relieved to be here, where she was alone, where it was quiet, where she could rest. She was weary, and sleep was her only reprieve from this battered existence, the only kindness in her beaten-down life.

She pulled a thin blanket up to her shoulders and stretched her ankles from side to side. Sleep, she told herself. She knew she must get sleep before having to get back out there, before having to earn more money in the only work she had ever known: selling her body, and her dignity in the process.

But a few hours of sleep was all she got; in fact, she was startled awake by the shouts of people in the street. She moaned as she rolled over, trying to block the noise from her ears. Her head pounded. Her joints stiffened. The shouts grew into screams, and before long she could not sleep at all from the commotion that now sounded as if it were under her window.

She pressed her thumb and fingers into her neck again, pushing away her long black hair, and she listened as the crowd tossed around words like waves in a storm: something about a rabbi coming through town, a man who helped others. Something about going to a leader's home, as well as rumors of an uprising or healing or chaos. It was hard to make out exactly what the crowd was saying, and the woman lay still in the dark, longing for the safety of rest, wanting the people simply to go away.

"He gave me back my boy!" a woman outside suddenly exclaimed, loud and sure and hopeful. The words fell on her ears with urgency, and she groaned. She opened her eyes and strained to listen. These were new sounds to her, emotions she had not remembered for many years. Anxious, tired eyes explored the dark until again the woman outside proclaimed the news: "It's true, he gave me back my son, my son who was dead!"

At that, the woman sat up from her bed and pushed open the window. Again the sun pierced her eyes as she squinted out onto the street below, following the voice to a widow, a grateful face with an eager young man beside her. Could it be?

Could it be there was such a man who cared so deeply for a mother's grief? A man who would give to a woman rather than take?

A soft breeze melted her doubt, and she watched as the mother held her son close to her, laughing and shouting with a mysterious joy. From the window, the woman glanced across the other faces below and wondered how one man could stir such feeling, such confusion. But the mother and son were certain, it seemed to her, and that was when something snapped in her tired soul. She watched the crowd wander through the street and around the corner, the mother laughing and the others yelling. And somehow she knew she could not let them get far.

She pulled the window half shut, allowing the sun to stream into her room. Then she turned to the table, grabbed the bowl, and threw off the lid. Her hands shook now with a strange blend of fear and hope that she had all but forgotten she could feel. As she poured the coins from the bowl, she counted the savings that lay before her. Almost enough to get her somewhere else. At least two years of work glistened there in the morning light: two years of hatred and shame and abandoned love offered in the heat of too many men's lust. Two years of bitterness and guilt at the hands of drunken violations.

It was all she had, and it was all she needed.

She threw her dress back on and tied her purse to her waist. The coins jiggled as she hurried out the door, head still aching, bones still sore, hair still bouncing on her shoulders. She could not remember a time when her body did not ache, so much so she had come to believe it was normal, it was how life would always be. Pain and exhaustion were as common as the work she did each night at the hands of angry men. Heartaches and loveless sex the only memories or visions she had anymore. Yes, the degrading toil had stolen her hope, pushing her deeper into a world of shame. After all, who did not know what she was?

How was it, then, that something the widow exclaimed pulled her from her restless sleep and into the city—though she was not sure what drove her so. Perhaps it was the young man's face that moved her. Or perhaps the mere possibility that a man could give at all pushed her from her room, onto the morning street, and toward the market. She needed to know.

The sun was approaching the middle of the sky now, and the woman's eyes stung again from the light. Still, she blinked and hurried and elbowed her way to the market. When she saw it, she would somehow know what she needed to buy, what she must spend her savings on. Though she was not sure what she was looking for, she felt compelled to find it. No, she felt wooed, drawn, that was the difference, as if her life depended on it, as if she would never know rest otherwise.

Dead chickens hung across racks, and purses, bottles, and blankets lined the streets. Someone yelled for fish, another for apples and bread. There were jars in one stall, woven cloths at another, and pans beside them. The woman's eyes jumped from item to item, her legs struggling to keep up as she walked through the center of the market. Her already sore neck was pinched as she looked back and forth, and she kept an anxious hand across her waist. Some people moved away as she approached, casting their eyes from her long black hair to her tired face, and mumbling under their breath. This morning, though, she did not have the energy to care. This morning, their stares could not distract her.

Then she saw it. A few feet away at an artist's table were three, maybe four, rows of colored jars made of marble and stone. In the middle was a tall rose-colored jar, with slight curves and tiny thin designs running up and down. The sun seemed to brighten the pink colors. She went to touch it, but the vendor stopped her and told her the price. The woman—never taking her eyes from the rose marble jar—reached in her purse and grabbed the coins. She dropped them in the man's palm and picked up the jar.

It had been a long time since she had held such beauty in her hands, since she had felt such smooth, textured loveliness. She sighed a breath of dignity but only for a moment as the vendor waved her on.

With her jar held close to her chest, she turned toward the other end of the market, the place where they sold incense and balms and perfumes. She moved quickly through the crowd, now more than certain what she needed but still not sure what drove her on. She arrived at a table with lines of incense smoke clouding the air. She took her rose marble jar, handed it to a white-haired man who sold perfumes, and asked him to fill her jar. He stared at her as if he could not believe what she was asking: did she know how much it would cost to fill this jar with perfume?

It did not matter, she whispered, looking toward the ground. He demanded to see her money first, and when she showed him the remaining coins in her purse, he took the jar from the tired woman and poured in a strong lovely liquid. The aroma sank into her soul, and again she felt different. She watched the man seal the jar, gather up her entire savings, and drop every last one of her coins into his already fat purse. Her cheeks formed a small smile—a most unfamiliar thing—until he pushed her away from his business and into the market's frenzy.

Now she held the marble jar even tighter as she hurried to the crowd that had gathered under her window. A stocky man brushed against her, admiring her flowing hair and pretty face, and muttered to her in a low voice how he wanted her to come with him. But she shook her head and kept walking, firmly, quickly. And then the man cursed her as she hurried by.

Finally, she found the crowd several streets ahead, and she stepped into the throng of anxious people to hear what they were saying. More rumors, more confusion about the strange teacher—or was he a rabbi?—who'd given a widow her son. The woman struggled to make sense of what she heard, and asked an elderly woman standing beside her what was happening. Yes, one of the leaders was throwing the rabbi a feast, she said, at his home outside of town, and several other teachers and leaders would be coming. That's what she had heard, at least, and it had already begun. Why did she want to know? Surely, she was not thinking of going, was she? Not someone like her?

The sun dropped further in the sky, and the woman's head still ached from sleeplessness. She slipped away from the crowd, and with both hands tight around the jar she kept walking through the town, past buildings, houses, and synagogues, past the district where she worked, and along the dirt road that led outside of town. The muscles in her neck throbbed, and her mind traced the events of the day. She began questioning what she was about to do. What had she been thinking? Why wasn't she back at her room, trying to sleep and get ready for another long night of work? What in the world would happen if she followed through with this idea?

But as she glanced down at the jar again, she knew she could not turn back. Its splendor lifted her heart, its smell nourished her hope. She kept walking.

And when dusk sprinkled its way across the clouds, the woman stopped outside a house. She heard laughter and loud voices echo through the courtyard. A few men came up suddenly behind her, eyeing her suspiciously, and yet whisking past her into the house. She heard one say something about the teacher, and when she knew she was at the right place, she gathered up her courage and walked straight ahead.

No one greeted her at the door; instead, she moved invisibly past the groups of people, past the tables of fruit, wine, and fish. Her eyes searched the men's faces in the room: leaders, rabbis, religious officials, fishermen, business managers, all talking and arguing like students in a school. Some she'd done business with, she thought. She did not like being around so many men, so many low voices, and felt a tinge of fear contract in her neck because of the sheer number of men present. When no one stopped to question her, she waited in a corner and tried to imagine what might happen next. She could not.

Until she saw his face. Gentleness beckoned in his eyes, compassion spilled from his smile. This *had* to be the man who gave the widow back her son, the teacher who healed the sick and helped the hurting. He walked through the same door she had just come in, and the owner of the house quickly ushered him to the center of the room. As she watched him move—his hand resting on one man's shoulders, his eyes soothing another's soul—her heart jumped to see his light. It was true! There *was* a man who would give and not take from her, who would love and not lust for her, who would honor and not harm her.

For the first time that day, her eyes stung, not from the terrible sunlight against her darkness, but from the presence that shone before her. Emotions long forgotten pushed against her soul, against every inch of her being, and she could not, would not, fight the tears.

Then the beautiful rose-colored jar of perfume seemed to pull the woman to the man's feet. She began to sob and wail as one whose heart is being crushed and caressed at the same time. She removed the seal from her jar, poured the elegant ointment across the rabbi's bare feet, and ran her fingers slowly over his toes and ankles and heels. Her tears mixed lightly into the costly perfume, and both washed the sand from his feet. She could not contain herself. She leaned over and pressed her lips to his toes.

To her amazement, never once did he stop her tears, never once did he resist her kiss, and never once did he demand a single thing from her.

She knelt beside the now-empty marble jar, aroma calming the air like rain on a summer morning. And then she did something no one with any social morals would have expected, something no woman like her would ever do unless she was working: she took her long flowing black hair—the same hair that had won over men on moonlit nights—gathered it to one side, and brushed it across the tops of the teacher's wet feet. Back and forth, back and forth the hair stroked his feet as the woman continued to sob. Her shoulders shook in the breaking. Her heart ached in the hoping.

What she did not know was how utterly aghast the host had become, not only at the sight of her disreputable presence but at the outrageous display of affection this woman was giving his honored guest. Obviously, she was still looking for business even in the midst of such an esteemed gathering. He found her repulsive. He made no bones about it either; his disgust was as public as her abominable gesture. And obviously, the rabbi was not a very principled leader since he was allowing a woman like her to touch him at all. No, the host of this feast was not impressed by the lack of discernment his guest displayed.

But he did not know who it was who'd come to his feast.

For then the rabbi did an equally strange thing: he told the host a story while the woman carried on. Instantly the dinner crowd was quiet: "Two men owed money to a certain moneylender. One owed him five hundred denarii, and the other fifty. Neither of them had the money to pay him back, so he canceled the debts of both. Now which of them will love him more?"

Except for the woman's cries, silence hung in the room, ready to burst like a rain cloud. Heads turned to the host and waited for his reply. He cleared his throat. The teacher looked at the woman. Then the host looked around the room and answered: "I suppose the one who had the bigger debt canceled." Eyes turned back to the man whose feet were being washed and kissed. No one moved.

"You have judged correctly." And with that he admonished the host for his bad manners—the woman had washed his feet with her tears though the host never once offered him a towel or basin to wash up. She offered him countless kisses, yet the host failed to greet him properly. She poured perfume across his dirty feet, yet the host had forgotten to bless him with the touch of oil. The owner of the house coughed again and was about to respond when the teacher continued: "Therefore, I tell you, her many sins have been forgiven—for she loved much. But he who has been forgiven little loves little."

Murmurs rose around the room, and faces looked askance across the crowd. Conversations and weights shifted. But again, the rabbi's kindness pierced the consciences of these influential people around the room, and they could not think of anything to say to him. So he gazed directly at the woman and spoke in a voice she had always yearned to hear from a man. His tenderness melted her shame, and his power served her need: "Your sins are forgiven. Your faith has saved you; go in peace."

And though none of the important men who heard him quite knew what to make of his comment or his claim to forgive such a sinner, the woman knew exactly what he meant.

She closed her eyes at the sound of freedom, a sound that swept through her body like the soft breeze of a new day, a better day. Oh, how glad she was to have spent all she had to find the one man who would give her more than she'd need.

And now, finally, gratefully, she breathed in the dignity he offered, rubbed her eyes, and walked back through the city to her room, where she fell into the deepest, sweetest sleep she had ever known.

### The Context

To imagine the woman of tears is to feel the deep sense of release that comes when you recognize the extent of your darkness and are offered light anyway. It is the true story of what happens when your sin is all you—and everyone else—sees and yet you are pardoned from it. You cannot help but weep in gratitude with all that you are. Deep-felt forgiveness, Jesus said, created deep and tender love. It was the reason the woman could climb from the depths of her despair and into a life that was truly life!

Up until this exchange, Jesus had been walking the roads of Judea, responding uniquely to the needs of the people. Yes, he'd healed the sick (Luke 4:38–40), cast out evil spirits (4:31–36), restored sight to the blind (7:21), and of course, brought a dead son back to life for his mother. He'd preached good news to the poor (4:18–19) and completely disrupted the status quo of the religious leaders who were not expecting the Messiah to act or speak quite like this (6:11).

But for all the great miracles he'd performed, for all the lives he'd transformed and words of comfort he'd given, he'd only once offered forgiveness to someone—a paralytic man who was literally dropped through the ceiling by his friends in front of Jesus (5:17–26). Never had Jesus extended radical grace and absolution in such an intimate way as he did to this woman who'd probably just the night before slept with several men so she could pay her rent.

This was, well, upsetting—especially for the Pharisee who'd invited Jesus to come have dinner in his home. Pharisees were members of a conservative Jewish sect, devout adherents of the law found both in the Torah and in the oral tradition known as the Mishna. Considering the context of the Pharisee, it is understandable that he would not have invited a "woman who had lived a sinful life in that town." It was equally understandable that he would have found her actions with his honored guest both inappropriate and unacceptable. She was not supposed to be there, doing this, and because Jesus had done nothing to stop her, the Pharisee was not at all acting out of character to question the visiting rabbi's leadership skills.

But we know by now that Jesus was more concerned with extending compassion than he was with observing the law; he was more interested in providing grace than in commending self-righteous works. There was something uniquely different about him.

Because of that difference and at great risk, the woman decided to crash the Pharisee's party. She'd even brought an expensive alabaster jar filled with expensive perfume—both of which would have cost her more money than anything she'd ever purchased. Yet she brought the jar, along with her emotional baggage and undeniable gratitude, for one solitary purpose: to serve Jesus. *He* became the object of her very public display of affection and devotion. But in so doing, she was also compromising Christ's reputation as a "prophet," offending the religious experts of the culture.

### The Conflict

Her mere presence and her strange actions, of course, created instant tension in the Pharisee's home. She must have been excruciatingly desperate to put herself in such a place, but as Charles Spurgeon said, "These are not the tears of sentimental emotion, but a rain of holy heart—sorrow for her sin."[2] She was genuinely grieving over her life, exposed by the character of Jesus and willing to risk all she had for this moment of release.

Her repentance contrasted sharply with the Pharisee's self-righteousness, and Jesus, master teacher that he was, was not only pleased by her humility but saw it as an extraordinarily teachable moment. He would confront the deception of human piety by elevating the absolute abandon that came with holy forgiveness.

When he finished his sermon illustration about debtors, and the Pharisee got the answer right, Jesus ignored the man and instead turned to the woman. "Your faith has saved you," he said. Everyone there must have been wondering, what faith? She'd poured expensive perfume from a beautiful jar across his feet, washed his feet with her tears, and dried them with her hair. Where was the faith in that?

He did not say, however, that her humility had saved her, or her repentance or even her tears. It was her faith that saved her: the courageous and desperate faith she had for risking the public scorn of religious leaders as she expressed her love for Jesus. Faith was jumping into something where she didn't know what would happen, but she believed Someone was worth the risk. Such an honest and vulnerable step was a step toward freedom.

Her whole spirit and soul became so absorbed by Jesus, her vision so fixed on him alone and not on anyone around the Pharisee's house, that she could not help but serve him. She had nothing to lose and everything to gain. And so she gave and loved him with an abandon unmatched by others.

But when the Pharisee complained about her under his breath, Christ confronted him by publicly defending the woman. He set her as a model before the Pharisee and the other male religious leaders, thereby restoring the dignity that had been stolen in her "profession," affirming the newness of her life, and granting her the peace she'd always hoped for.

## The Counsel

Because she was honest, willing, and focused in her repentance, Jesus allowed her to perform a lowly but common courtesy for him that the Pharisee hadn't bothered with. His feet needed washing. It was a dusty place, and who knew when he'd have another chance to clean up. He never once saw himself as above the woman, never tried to stop her, but received from her an offering of sincere sorrow and gratitude. He accepted her ministry to him. He affirmed her in the process.

Accepting the gifts and help of others is not easy for us, especially westerners who—like the Pharisee—like to keep control of situations and manage each element and guest in our lives. But because this woman gave so extravagantly of herself and the perfume, Jesus was only too glad to accept such a gift from her.

And he does the same for us, inviting us to bring our shame and pasts and holy sorrow to his feet so that he might restore us as he did the woman, so that he might cleanse us with his forgiveness. As C. S. Lewis described it, "The precious alabaster box which one must break over the Holy Feet is one's heart. Easier said than done. And the contents become perfume only when it is broken. While they are safe inside they are more like sewage. All very alarming."[3]

How could God's Son, the prophet from Nazareth, sit so peacefully with the woman whose heart was breaking? Because he knew that his heart too would break for the sins of his people. He too would weep over Jerusalem, over the wayward choices his people would make. And he would cry out to his heavenly Father on the cross in our stead, so that we—like the woman—could live lives full of dignity, acceptance, and restoration.

### The Conversion

And so, a woman of tears became a woman of comfort and new freedom. A woman plagued by guilt and shame was changed into one of dignity and grace, released into the joy of service. As Jesus accepted the only offering she had to give him—a broken heart—he then astonished everyone at the Pharisee's house by saying that such desperate gifts were exactly what he was looking for. Those were the offerings he would accept, but those who lived in the illusion of their own self-competence would know little about grace and the power of forgiveness.

Only when we recognize we're drowning, when we're flailing and sobbing and gulping the bitterness of the salty water, do we cry out for help. No, it doesn't take much imagination to know we need saving. It just takes an honest admission that we cannot save ourselves, an admission that moves us once again to watch in our mind's eyes the blood sprayed across the flesh of God's Son. Imagining his tears and pain for our sakes can't help but woo us.

## In-Between Reflection

1. How did the gift of your imagination affect your reading of this story?

2. The woman who came forward to wash Jesus's feet with her tears experienced immense shame and guilt throughout her life. Yet Jesus held her up as a model to the religious leaders there. Why?

3. In fact, Jesus *allowed* the woman to bring him her tears and to serve him by washing his feet with expensive perfume from her jar. What do you learn about Jesus from his response, and how does this apply to your life?

4. Can you recall a time when someone made a very public declaration of faith in Jesus, one that might have felt "uncomfortable" for others at the time? What happened? What did you learn from it?

5. What do you think it means to contemporary women and men that the woman's "many sins have been forgiven—for she loved much"?

6. Apply that same statement to your life, as you consider the many ways you've experienced forgiveness. How has forgiveness changed you? How could God help you extend it to others? How has it increased your capacity to love?

## Digging Deeper

Every person lives with some regret or is familiar with shame. We make bad choices that later in our lives force us to wonder what we were thinking. Yet the hope of the gospel and the theme of the Bible is that God stands waiting for us to return to him for forgiveness. He wants us to repent of our sins, to cry over our mistakes, but also to accept the grace and forgiveness he provided through the death of Jesus Christ. The reality of the Christian life is not that we will stop sinning as long as we're in these bodies, but that our sin no longer defines us, that God's love through Christ's blood has covered over us and made us new creatures. Examine the following verses in light of the woman who washed Christ's feet with her tears: Jeremiah 31:15–20, Luke 15:1–10, and Revelation 21:4. What new insights do these passages give you regarding sorrow over our sin and the freedom of forgiveness?

You might consider looking anew at the story of Peter's denial of Christ (John 18:25–27) and Christ's gracious reinstatement of his identity and ministry (John 21:15–25) to further understand Christ's response to our shame.

# PREPARATION

### The Faith of a Syrophoenician Woman

[24]Jesus left that place and went to the vicinity of Tyre. He entered a house and did not want anyone to know it; yet he could not keep his presence secret. [25]In fact, as soon as she heard about him, a woman whose little daughter was possessed by an evil spirit came and fell at his feet. [26]The woman was a Greek, born in Syrian Phoenicia. She begged Jesus to drive the demon out of her daughter.

[27]"First let the children eat all they want," he told her, "for it is not right to take the children's bread and toss it to their dogs."

[28]"Yes, Lord," she replied, "but even the dogs under the table eat the children's crumbs."

[29]Then he told her, "For such a reply, you may go; the demon has left your daughter."

[30]She went home and found her child lying on the bed, and the demon gone.

MATTHEW 15:21—29

### The Faith of the Canaanite Woman

[21]Leaving that place, Jesus withdrew to the region of Tyre and Sidon. [22]A Canaanite woman from that vicinity came to him, crying out, "Lord, Son of David, have mercy on me! My daughter is suffering terribly from demon-possession."

[23]Jesus did not answer a word. So his disciples came to him and urged him, "Send her away, for she keeps crying out after us."

²⁴He answered, "I was sent only to the lost sheep of Israel."

²⁵The woman came and knelt before him. "Lord, help me!" she said.

²⁶He replied, "It is not right to take the children's bread and toss it to their dogs."

²⁷"Yes, Lord," she said, "but even the dogs eat the crumbs that fall from their masters' table."

²⁸Then Jesus answered, "Woman, you have great faith! Your request is granted." And her daughter was healed from that very hour.

### Jesus Feeds the Four Thousand

²⁹Jesus left there and went along the Sea of Galilee. Then he went up on a mountainside and sat down.

When you are ready, continue reflecting on the following question:

Perhaps you've read this story before. What new insights or observations jumped out to you as you read her story anew in this Gospel account? Jot them down. Take a few moments to reflect before reading chapter 7.

**Prayer:** *Gracious God, thank you that you do not treat us as we deserve but offer us the surprising adventure of life with you in Christ! Amen.*

---
7
---

# Hustling for Scraps

"I am not," she said tearfully, "a wart hog. From hell." But the denial had no force.

Flannery O'Connor, *Revelation*

I first met Percy Talbot a few years ago on the corner of 68th and Broadway in New York City. Pushing stringy brown hair out of her face, she lit a cigarette and spoke in a rough Kentucky drawl about life in prison. I listened to her story; I had to. There was something soft in her toughness, a buried pain that surfaced every now and then on her otherwise youthful face. Yes, she'd done some terrible things. She'd been disgraced, pushed aside, and put down on every level as a result. But she said she was just hoping for a new start in a new place where there was "enough country around to lose yourself in." She hadn't belonged much of anywhere before and simply wanted somewhere, someday to do right.

I smiled and found myself cheering for Percy in her new endeavor, wanting it indeed to be the soothing ointment her tender and bruised soul seemed to yearn for. But for the next seventy-five minutes or so, I watched instead as her raw persistence made *her* the balm, albeit scratchy and rough, for the unsuspecting people in Gilead, Maine. And in New York City.

When I walked into Percy's life in the film *The Spitfire Grill*, I forgot I was in the Sony theater on New York's Upper West Side. I had been intrigued with the film's history since the *Wall Street Journal* had given it front-page coverage. It seemed a little Catholic parish in the Mississippi Delta—a religion and region not often covered in a New York newspaper—wanted to raise some money for their ministry with the rural poor while simultaneously communicating Judeo-Christian values to the culture. They figured a movie could accomplish both, so they found *The Spitfire Grill* (written by a Jewish screenwriter) and recruited most of the actors and crew to work pro bono. Their mission was accomplished, in fact, so much so that the movie won wide acclaim at film festivals and earned enough money during the weekend it opened in theaters around the country that they built their new school in the Delta. And then some.

But it wasn't the story behind the story that kept me in my seat—although it initially got me there. It was the real people I saw on the screen, the kind who lived and breathed and ached for lifetimes in the same place with the same faces, thinking the same thoughts until they died. The "small-town-ness" of Gilead, Maine, made life numb and ordinary until something extraordinary stepped into their world and provided them a peek at perspective.

Enter Perchance (Percy) Talbot. Upon release from serving a five-year sentence for manslaughter—which she doesn't keep a secret—Percy (astutely portrayed by Alison Elliott) arrives in Gilead tough, afraid, and cautiously hopeful. Immediately, she's aware that her strange presence does not fit neatly into this little town where folks have been born and raised and died for generations. Why Gilead? She read about it in prison and was drawn to its open country, to the fact it had "roots so deep you couldn't tear 'em out from them."

A curmudgeon widow named Hannah Ferguson (played beautifully by Ellen Burstyn) owns the town diner and is getting older and crankier each day she has to run it. She needs to hire some help for the diner but isn't thrilled when the sheriff suggests she employ this stranger, this ex-con. She relents, though, when she realizes she doesn't have many choices, and Percy gets the job as a waitress. The whole town—which gathers daily at the Spitfire—is clearly shaken by the funny talk and shady past of this woman who's now serving them eggs.

When Hannah falls, breaks her hip, and is forced to rest, Percy is thrust into her first role as healer, disrupting the status quo by dishing up half cooked pancakes and burnt bacon. (Healing never tastes good initially.) Until Shelby Goddard, the wife of Hannah's only nephew and the story's antagonist, Nahum, picks up the spatula to help Percy run the Spitfire. While Hannah recovers, the two become friends by default, and Percy learns from Shelby (played by the gifted Marcia Gay Harden) about Hannah's source of crankiness and grief: the loss of her son, Eli, a town hero sacrificed in the Vietnam war.

Percy's battered innocence and awkward gratitude give Shelby renewed purpose and respect. At the same time, Hannah's physical pain and sudden neediness invite Percy to serve out of her own brokenness and desperation to belong. The redemptive process emerging for these three women becomes both uniquely personal and significantly interdependent. While rubbing ointment on Hannah's leg, Percy asks *the* question of the story, "Do you suppose if a  wound goes real deep the healing of it can hurt almost as bad as what caused it?"

The answer is both inevitable and a sign of what's to come.

Once Hannah is back on her feet, she decides the Spitfire isn't worth the trouble for a woman her age. Since it's been on the market for years and hasn't sold, Percy and Shelby convince her to sponsor an essay contest to *give* it away so she can retire comfortably. Essays with one-hundred-dollar entry fees come from across the country in hopes of winning the small cafe. So many, in fact, that town residents have to help out by reading the letters as well, and in the process remember that there is a world of pain and hope beyond theirs.

But the contest turns sour as talk of fear and stolen money bring damaging suspicions, in particular to one ex-con. Those of us watching Percy's life at this point as well as the reaction of Gilead to the rumor mill are slapped with the sin of our own skepticism and arrogance. As Shelby tells Hannah how "Percy's damning herself for a past that would have killed you or me," we know something terrible is about to happen.

Still, the outsider never quits. She's determined to find a better way.

The stakes are raised as truth finally floats to the surface: we learn the horror of Percy's incestuous past, the death of her child, and the ensuing murder of her abusive stepfather. Though her confession brings freedom, it is not without its cost, as it rarely is in real life either. An unexpected horror happens with Hannah's money, yet somehow, miraculously, good is born from the ensuing tragedy. Redemption triumphs—so much so that usually snobby New York audiences clapped, cried, or cheered as the credits rolled on the screen.

Even now I'm pulled by Percy's demise because she has become for me an example of integrity in brokenness, honest weakness, gutsy resolve. I hear her singing on the mountain, "There is a balm in Gilead to make the wounded whole. There is a balm in Gilead to heal the weary soul," and I want to believe her. I remember Percy the other times I've "met" her in my life: in the tears of a friend who cried over another's pain, in the sheer doggedness of a cancer-stricken relative, in the tender care of a mother on welfare who insisted on cooking dinner for me. I like Percy because she reminds me that shame and pride are never worth holding on to, and that my capacity to experience wonder and joy are directly proportional to how I confront pain and grief, that both make living worthwhile.

Both lead me to another Balm in another Gilead.

And so, *The Spitfire Grill* became for me a most alluring film. It is not a religious movie—the Catholic Mississippians who made it would never want it to be limited to that category. Nor is it a woman's movie; though its main characters are women, the challenges and emotions transcend gender stereotypes.

Instead, it is a well-written film about what happens when a woman is desperate enough to risk giving herself away. It's a story of what it means to live beyond brokenness and shame, to accept who you are, past and all, so you can move forward. And it is a redemptive tale, one where trees thought to be worthless become a medicinal source; a missing son is reconciled with his lamenting mother; a neglected wife discovers her worth; an empty church becomes filled; and a hollow, lifeless town learns to accept outsiders.

All because a cigarette-smoking, stringy-haired ex-con went looking for a new start.

## A Woman of Humiliation

The character of Percy is still so endearing to me that I confess I get teary when I watch the video (one of the few I own) or think of her story. Her raw pain and unselfish perspective move me and challenge me. Especially in an age when weakness is too often hidden behind illusions of reputations and professionalism, Percy's realness is both refreshing and encouraging. For who of us can live up to the masks our culture pressures us into wearing?

I suspect most of us want to learn what it means to live honestly with the sorrows and regrets in our lives. We are tired of being held captive to them and authentically want the freedom to be ourselves, to start over in a place where the pressure is off. We want to live in that place where the power of the past is broken with the possibility of a new life, a new hope, a new family of friends who accept us no matter what. Usually, though, it is only when we become desperate enough, when we have run out of our own resources to rely on, that we go searching for such change.

But we only need to look again to Scripture to find the encouragement we need to set out on such a journey. In fact, we meet this same kind of woman when we come to the strange little story of the Syrophoenician—or Canaanite—woman found in Matthew 15:21–29 and Mark 7:24–30. This marginalized woman was a desperate, probably exhausted, mother who had been caring for some time for a daughter who'd been "disturbed" by a demon. That in itself might have caught Christ's attention, except that this woman also had a past, more specifically, a bad history. She was a Greek and a pagan whose ancestors were from the land of Canaan, a clan of folks who had long been enemies of Israel and Jews. In other words, she was an outsider ethnically, spiritually, and personally. Still, her little girl was taunted by demons, and there's not much a mother won't do to alleviate her child's suffering.

So she acted on her instincts: she went to the man whom she'd heard had been healing sick people, feeding hungry masses, restoring cripples, and preaching good news to anyone who'd listen. She just wanted to find a place, really, where she and her daughter could start anew, where they could move on from the ostracizing they received from their community and the abuse they endured (in different ways) from the demons. She wanted freedom. And though she knew she was not "one of his people," that she was clearly an outcast, what she'd heard about this man meant she at least had to try.

In her gritty Gentile way, she bothered the rabbi and his followers with a favor. Help, really—anything to let her start over, to pick up the pieces, to restore her child. She didn't mind admitting who she was, and she wasn't about to quit until she experienced the redemptive hand of the man she was clearly interrupting.

It was just the type of raw and unpretentious faith Jesus was looking for.

## The Context

Because of the story's placement in the two Gospel accounts, it's helpful to look at what's happened before and what happens after to better appreciate its significance. There's no question this story is the type of passage my pastor calls "hard candy"—the kind you need to suck on for a while to fully appreciate all its flavors.

Jesus had just left the predominately Jewish territory of Galilee, where the crowds had gathered around him, pressing him for help. Now, he needed time to rest with and teach his disciples. Both Matthew and Mark place this story right after Jesus's discussion on Jewish purity as if to imply that this unclean Gentile woman was about to push the point. The disciples were clearly bothered by her presence, and it seems at first glance that Jesus was too. Why was this unwelcome outsider being allowed to interrupt their down time? Hadn't they come north intentionally to a less "public" place for a little R and R?

In spite of their plans, the disciples and Jesus were nonetheless visitors themselves in Gentile country. Immediately following the woman's gutsy interaction with him, Christ went on to miraculously feed four thousand with only a few loaves of bread and fish. The placement of her story was not accidental in that the exchange between Jesus and the "unholy" woman used food as a metaphor. It was as if somehow this woman knew that this rabbi had access to plenty of sustenance, and she was determined to get even a crumb of it.

The cultural context was such that Jesus had been winning over the people but now was on new turf, seeking time first to regain some strength and instruct his disciples before moving on to reach these people. Matthew introduced this woman as a Canaanite because his largely Jewish audience would have immediately understood her history and its bitter significance for twelve Jewish men. Mark emphasized her birthplace in Syria because of the political implications it would have on his largely Roman audience.

So, when she crashed their retreat, begging Jesus to help her girl, she was clearly not welcomed. Not only was she "foreign" to them, but she was needy and pushy, disturbing their otherwise serene getaway. The disciples became so annoyed with her that they pressed their boss to get rid of her, to send her away so they could have a little peace. They didn't know what to do with such a strange woman and weren't about to accept her. Instead of telling her themselves, they put the job on Jesus.

In one of the only places in the Gospels where Jesus did not immediately respond to a need, he actually seemed to side with his friends. As if to say, "We don't have time right now for someone like you," he reminded her of his role: to offer salvation to God's chosen people.

## The Conflict

The tension must have been as thick in the air as it seemed in the diner the first morning Percy served eggs. For here was a desperate stranger, clearly not welcomed but nonetheless digging in her heels, determined to get what she came for. Her daughter was demonically harassed, Christ's followers wanted nothing to do with her, and the only man in the world she knew could help her was pushing her away.

"It is not right to take the children's bread and toss it to their dogs," Jesus actually said to her.

At first glance it seemed as if this rabbi who'd healed so many other needy mothers and children was not only brushing her off but also adding insult to injury. He all but called her a dog. It was the same Greek word Jews used for house pets. To continue the metaphor, Jews were the children, Greeks the little dogs that were kept indoors, not the type who ran free in the courtyards or fields. His odd comment seemed to suggest a hierarchy, reminding the woman of her place in the world. She was guilty by association, born into the wrong bloodline, destined for perpetual marginalization. Because we know nothing else of her life, there's no doubt Christ's comment seemed like salt in the wound, a kick in the teeth.

But things with Jesus were never as they seemed. And somehow, this woman understood that.

So without skipping a beat, without wanting to create more conflict by daring to take away from God's people what she knew was rightfully theirs, she pressed the Master in front of his friends. They couldn't believe she was still around. Obviously, she hadn't taken the hint very well and seemed sure to be provoking more insults. Yet, even as the woman heard Christ's comments and saw his followers' disdain, she instinctively responded. How? By first acknowledging his lordship—something his own disciples hadn't yet done—and then in the same gritty and inappropriate breath, making her case.

"Yes, Lord, but even the dogs eat the crumbs that fall from their masters' table."

The disciples' jaws must have dropped. Here was a broken pagan Gentile woman all but admitting her status as a "dog." She had not run off embarrassed and hurt. She was still standing there, not defending herself or getting angry and returning the insults. And she was not pretending to be someone she was not. She simply and unashamedly *agreed* with Christ's assessment of her "dog-ness," and then she had the guts to make her request anyway.

She was determined to get mercy from the teacher she knew had offered it to others. How could she demand such a thing from the Lord, knowing what the others were feeling about her, hearing the rabbi's apparent insult, and knowing, of course, her own past and exceedingly low status not only as a Gentile but as a Canaanite *and* a woman?

She *believed*. She believed even a crumb from Jesus was worth more than anything else in the world including her reputation—and far better than the life she'd been living so far. Even a crumb from this man could feed—and heal—her tormented daughter. And no amount of humiliation would convince her otherwise.

## The Counsel

Do we learn from this story that Jesus, the King of Kings and Lord of Lords, God Incarnate, really did have a mean streak in him after all? Does it teach us that if just the right person pushed his buttons he could indeed get nasty? Or are we to believe that all he'd done for others really was just an exclusive one-time "offer" and not available to the rest of the world?

Hardly. In fact, if we read this story in light of the rest of the book, that is, with the bigger picture of God's redemptive story in mind, we'll remember Jesus—who was both fully God and fully man—could not act inconsistently with his character. The one who had been preaching that God so loved the world that he gave his only Son could not suddenly change his mind. In fact, one commentator suggested that anyone who knew Jesus's genealogy would immediately recall how he had Canaanites in his own blood lineage. Matthew cites (in chapter 1:1–5) Old Testament *women* Tamar and Rahab—both of whom were Canaanites—as part of his heritage, emphasizing his theme that God's compassion extended to Jews and Gentiles alike. In other words, Jesus could never ultimately reject this woman for her ethnicity without also rejecting two of his own ancestors. Neither was possible for him as a man and as God in the flesh.

So what in the world was he doing when he made this apparently ethnically charged comment and what can we learn? First, instead of heeding his disciples' selfish request to send her away, instead of saying to them, "Yeah, you guys must be exhausted. I'll get rid of this pushy Greek lady," he started a conversation with her. Even by entering into a discussion with her, he was all but implying that there was something else on the horizon. Yes, he knew who she was and what she wanted, yet he did not send her away.

He did, however, respond with equal firmness to her insistence. Commentators agree that he was not cursing her, but he could have been suggesting her timing might not be right. She might have to wait for her request to be granted—and there is nothing wrong with waiting even though we live in a culture that operates as if waiting is the greatest tragedy we could experience.

He also might have been testing her—as well as his disciples—and so at first seemed reluctant to help. Maybe he wanted to make sure she understood his true mission and identity, lest as one commentator put it, "she treat him as one of the many wandering magicians to whom Gentiles sometimes appealed for exorcisms."

No matter how we look at it, or how Greeks might have responded to Jews at the time, one thing is clear: Jesus was acting—as he always did—in love. Certainly, he was the *only* one who had the authority and the grace to tell her who she really was, the only one who could put her in her place and remind her of her dependence. Why? Because he was keenly aware of her humanity and her needs, as he is with all of us.

Sometimes truth is exactly what we need to hear. Of course, not many of us like to be reminded that we are sinful, needy creatures, but when we hear the words from the Person we know is infinite love, absolute justice, and unending grace, the words become for us a soothing balm, one we apply to our aching hearts so we'll get moving in the right direction.

At my church in New York City, we often quote a saying from our pastor to one another: *we are more sinful than we ever want to admit and more loved than we dare to imagine.* The two truths must go together; otherwise, if we knew we were merely sinful without being loved, we would completely despair and walk away from life. But if we viewed God as merely a cuddly genie ready to serve our whims and fancies, without the cost real love or grace demands, we couldn't take our sins seriously.

With this in mind, Christ's words hit home. They were what she needed to hear first to confirm her obstinate faith in the King of the nation that conquered hers. As a result, her faith was too impressive for Jesus to ignore. So he exercised his authority in direct response to the desperate proclamation he'd just heard from her amazing comeback. "Yes, Lord, but even beggars like me and my daughter hustle the scraps of food from those above us."

She had no pretense, she played no games with Jesus, and so he responded to her unwavering belief and confidence in his ability to free her child. Hadn't he extended grace and salvation to others? Surely he was not about to change his tune.

No, he was not. And is not. Jesus still longs for each of us to come to him honestly, acknowledging our burdens, needs, limits, and weaknesses to him and allowing his light to expose us for who we are. He knows we cannot pretend to be spiritual, to be good or moral women or men, or to be other than what he has made us in this life he has given us. He invites us to his table, to partake of his presence, to worship him as the Lord of Lords with a raw and unpretentious acceptance of his power at work *in* us.

Like the woman, most of us don't really want much. Only a crumb that might fall to the floor for the poor unworthy creature we know deep down we really are. Besides, it was not for her only that she begged but mostly for her daughter, someone even more vulnerable than she.

How could he say no? Especially when he knew he would soon bear the ultimate humiliation on the cross for her sake, for the sake of all us beggars looking for bread. He, too, would be tormented, cast aside for her—and us—and for every other sinful, tormented child, regardless of ethnicity, history, or status. His gift of life—found in his sacrificial death—was to be a gift for all with the integrity to admit who they are and to believe who he is.

## The Conversion

This Gentile woman's confession of her own status in the light of Christ's was so real, so admirable, that Jesus did not even need to see her daughter in order to free her! When he heard the woman's comment, he must have stepped back, smiled, scratched his beard, and nodded his head. For he then responded to her by publicly affirming her honesty: "Woman, you have great faith! Your request is granted." Mark recorded his comment as "For such a reply, you may go; the demon has left your daughter."

Then the woman did another amazing thing: she believed Jesus. Rather than sticking around and begging him some more, imposing on his time with his disciples, she instead took him at his word, wiped her tears, and hurried home. There, Mark wrote, she found her child lying on the bed, and the demon gone. It had been a long, long time since the mother had seen her daughter look like this: so free, awake, and alive, no longer captive to darkness. There must have been tears and shouts and laughter and dancing at that homecoming!

Not only did she initially believe Jesus could meet her request, but she continued to believe him when he said her daughter was free! When she persistently stayed in his presence, admitted her own inability to do anything but beg for mercy, and reminded God that she believed in his power, her request was granted. Her daughter literally was changed. From that point on, their lives were never the same. A woman of humiliation had become a woman of confidence. A woman of torment now experienced the joy of absolute freedom. The gospel that was a tragedy, now was more than a comedy—it was a dream that had come true.

And with any transformation, others couldn't help but be affected. It's not hard to imagine how many people the woman must have told about the man who'd delivered her daughter from the demons that disturbed her. The neighbors must have heard all the commotion, hurried over, and then jumped into the dance line to kick up the rug with her and the healed girl!

Good news, indeed, is hard to keep a secret. For as Edith Deen wrote, this woman "no doubt went forth and spread her faith among others and paved the way for the Christian community at Tyre."[1] How do we know? Thirty years later Paul visited the same place on one of his missionary trips, as Acts 21:2–5 confirmed: "We found a ship crossing over to Phoenicia, went on board and set sail. After sighting Cyprus and passing to the south of it, we sailed on to Syria. We landed at Tyre, where our ship was to unload its cargo. Finding the disciples there, we stayed with them seven days. . . . But when our time was up, we left and continued on our way. All the disciples and their wives and children accompanied us out of the city, and there on the beach we knelt to pray."

In other words, what had once been a dry Gentile pagan land—the area where the Syrophoenician woman hustled and knelt and pleaded with the Lord to heal her daughter, the place where she interrupted his disciples and dug in her heels—became a thriving community where others believed with equally tenacious faith. God's redemptive story told again and again.

All because a feisty, desperate Canaanite mother went looking for a new start.

# In-Between Reflection

1. How did the story of *The Spitfire Grill* affect you and prepare you for the story of this outsider woman who interrupts Jesus and his followers? (You might consider renting the movie to review its message.)

2. What do the disciples' attitudes suggest to you about responding to those in need, and how does their attitude contrast with Christ's?

3. How did this story challenge you in thinking about people different from you?

4. What does the Canaanite woman teach you about prayer?

5. Is it difficult for you to admit your weaknesses or to confess who you really are? Why or why not?

6. What does Christ's response to this woman's personal confession of her status and her persistence for him to heal her daughter teach you about his character and desire for you?

# DIGGING DEEPER

No matter who we are, what family or class we're born into, all of us are unworthy to receive God's grace. Yet God has made it available to all through the life, death, and resurrection of Christ. He is eager to enter into a life-giving relationship with anyone bold and desperate enough to come and ask him. Examine the following verses in light of the story of the Syrophoenician woman: Jeremiah 29:10–14, 33:3, 1 Peter: 2:23–25, and Paul's testimony in 1 Timothy 1:12–17. What do each of these stories suggest about our worthiness and God's character?

What other Bible stories remind you of the theme of pursuing God with determination, tenacity, and longing until we get what we ask for (Jacob's wrestling, Daniel's discipline, etc.)?

# PREPARATION

Reflect for a few moments on the following verse and its significance for you in light of all we've explored in the stories of these nameless women.

 Jesus Christ is the same yesterday and today and forever.

Hebrews 13:8

When you are ready, continue reflecting on the following question:

Perhaps you've read this verse before. What new insights or implications does it have for you as it relates to the stories we've just explored? Jot them down.

Take a few moments to reflect before reading the epilogue.

**Prayer:** *"You wonderfully created, Almighty God, and yet more wonderfully You restored the dignity of our human nature; Grant that we who remember the story of the One You sent, the One who humbled himself to share in our humanity, may come to share in his divine life. For Christ's sake. Amen."*

A Collect for the Seasons

# EPILOGUE

## A DESPERATE TRUTH

Things are not perfect, because life is not TV and we are
real people with scarred, worried hearts.

Anne Lamott, *Plan B: Further Thoughts on Faith*

I picked up my husband last night from the airport. He had
been traveling on a business trip, and I have to confess that
when I found him waiting at the baggage claim carousel,
I was relieved. It wasn't that he'd been gone for months;
it had only been a weekend and two connecting flights. I
was relieved because I knew that a million different things
could have happened to prevent such a reunion. The plane
might not have landed, his health might not have served
him, the shuttle that took him to the airport from his hotel
could have been in an accident, and as for all the other dark
and dreary events that might have kept us apart, well, I
didn't dare imagine.

I do not mean to sound fatalistic. I only know that in those moments whenever I go to the airport to pick up my husband, or whenever he picks me up after I've spent a weekend teaching at a retreat, we offer each other probably the least guarded and truest face we have in our relationship. Our daily pressures are temporarily forgotten, our defenses are down, and our caution is pushed aside. It is a moment of recognition, I suppose, that our lives really are not our own, that we cannot begin to control what happens each day, and so, a reunion as simple as this in the terminal by the luggage becomes an absolute gift. We are together again. And we cannot take for granted even something so seemingly mundane as an airport arrival; we know nothing is guaranteed.

It's a desperate truth, really. A reckoning of the fact that we are mere mortals. We are not invincible. We are not in charge. We are frail, finite creatures, vulnerable to the laws of nature, in need of an infinite strength greater than ourselves.

Oh, how we want to believe otherwise.

But in the vulnerability of separation first and then reunion, we get a glimpse of the "might have beens," and consequently, our lack of ability to control them. It is true, after all, that our lives—like our world—are full of chaos and anxiety. We live in a time when people kill each other in war, families are torn apart, hurricanes (or tsunamis or earthquakes) devastate, and communities are crushed from it all. Marriages fail, cancer strikes, poverty cripples, and freak accidents happen. And if circumstances don't slap our cozy delusions to wake us up, bad choices and sinful responses will.

Any way we look at it, it can be a frightening thing, this thing called living. Everything seems up for grabs, and the stakes are always high because every day somewhere a man's passions have gone awry, a woman's dreams have been stolen, and a thousand other hearts and bodies have been bruised and battered by Mother Nature or dumb decisions or each other.

## The Bad News

Life really *is* hard.

We just aren't often aware of it. We live numbed and guarded lives of pretense and illusion, where we assume our spouses will return from a weekend trip and we do so in many ways because we live in a culture where such assumptions are taken for granted. Especially in western countries, we find a cultural addiction to comfortableness every time we turn around, and who of us is immune to it? I'll be the first to admit I like having a bed to sleep in each night, under a roof that doesn't leak, with a bathroom that has running water, and a refrigerator full of food. I'm glad there are clothes in my closet and drawers, a computer on my desk, and books on my shelves. Wanting to be comfortable is a normal thing; being addicted to it so much so that our days are ruined if our most basic necessity doesn't get met with bigger or better stuff, well, that can play tricks on our perspective. There's even an ancient word for it: *idolatry.*

Though our lifestyles might seem easy and comfortable—and they are, compared to how most of the world exists—our lives still are riddled with devastating crises and wrenching situations beyond our control. Authentic pain and heartache know no specific geography, history, class, or ethnicity. The poverty of the wealthy, Mother Teresa observed, is just as sad and despairing as third world poverty. Maybe more so, because as she said, it is a "poverty of the soul," one that is not easily "fixed."

The problem is we can't admit it. Or we don't like to. We know that we're both innately sinful and also made in

God's image, which, of course, is the tension of the human condition. British theologian John Stott calls it

> the paradox of humanness, that we are both breath of God and dust of earth, godlike and bestial, created and fallen, noble and ignoble. That seems to be why we both seek God and run away from him, both practice righteousness and suppress the truth in our unrighteousness, both recognize the claims of the moral law upon us and refuse to submit to it, both erect altars in God's honour and need to repent of our ignorance and sin.[1]

Most of us, though, want only to emphasize the "made in God's image" label of who we are. That sinful part is so messy, so confusing, so hard (especially for "self-made" Americans). So we hide behind the pretense—and the lie—of "togetherness." We believe we're not really so bad. And we'll even get better if we just take that class, or get this job or that relationship or a bigger house, or attend a different church, or have another child, because then we will have "it." We will finally be really "together" and satisfied. And so we keep guzzling down anything that will help us believe what we'd rather believe, anything that will plug the holes in our flimsy souls or numb the nightmares of our painful memories. Besides, when something doesn't work, we can always move on to the next thing. We have options. We can change the channel.

Or so we think.

Bob Dylan got it right when he sang: "You gotta serve somebody." We're wired to worship—and we can be absolutely sure all humans will indeed worship, every day of our lives! Make no mistake, we *will* serve someone or something. Period. Worship is who we are. And if we don't come at it honestly, we'll either throw in a substitute to bow before or put on a spiritual face as we offer our devotion to whatever tickles our fancy.

Because of this twenty-first-century illusion of self-sufficiency, I think these nameless women from the first century have all the more to teach us. Though we might have initially looked at their stories from a "modern" perspective, glancing over our shoulders as if we were more progressive or advanced, one particular theme has surfaced for me as I've prepared these chapters: we are no different. We are all thirsty for some purpose; we are all defective and unable to walk straight on our own. Each of us—no matter our status in life—is promiscuous, chasing after lovers we think will fulfill us. No matter how much is in our checkbooks, we are still shamefully poor when it comes to loving others. We grieve losses of all kinds and are much needier than we ever want to admit. And if you don't think this is true, try to remember how it felt the last time you had to ask someone for help.

Since I began teaching on these women's stories at retreats and while writing this book during the past year, several difficult circumstances occurred. The first was my hip replacement surgery and my recovery. Then the South Asian tsunami shattered our world. After that, two friends got really sick, car accidents happened, jobs were applied for and lost, and Christian business acquaintances began lying to me. The parents of a few close friends died suddenly, a neighbor began abusing her privileges as a tenant, the casualties increased in the Iraq war, and Hurricane Katrina hit—shattering us all over again. The news, the bills, the deadlines, the losses, and the pressures felt like they were piling up, and I internalized all of them. There were not many days, in fact, when I did not physically *feel* the confusion and pain of the events—in particular in a stress-related eye-muscle problem and a shoulder ache. Often, all I could think to pray was, "Lord, have mercy."

Then one morning it dawned on me: I was writing a book on *desperate women*. The more I wrote—and the more

I lived—the more qualified I began to feel! My need began to outweigh my natural resources, and I grew all the more aware of my inability to make sense of life on my own terms or through my own filter.

I needed the balm of a good story, one truer and greater than any I was experiencing. Still do. I needed these women to remind me how much I need Jesus, and still do. And the need just becomes deeper each day. It does not go away. As the apostle John wrote in his letter, "If we claim to be without sin, we deceive ourselves and the truth is not in us. If we confess our sins, he is faithful and just and will forgive us our sins and purify us from all unrighteousness" (1 John 1:8–9).

The point is not to wallow in our human hardships, despair, or grime, but to recognize first and foremost that we are humans with very real limitations—not superheroes with unbelievable powers. The truth is we do get grimy, filthy in fact, with no way of cleaning up our messes on our own. We can try, and Lord knows we do. But soon enough the filth—and the despair—will be back.

What we've missed somewhere along the way, however, is that there is no shame in being desperate. It is merely a state of being we're born into. It is just who we are. Call it a family trait, something we inherited in the Garden when the first human creatures suddenly became aware of their vulnerability. Yes, some of us are slower to recognize it than others. (I, for one, needed to write a book about it before I began to realize I was also writing about myself.)

But the truth is we *are* creatures in need, in process, on a journey toward getting help. None of us has arrived. And sometimes life throws us seasons of deeper desperation than at other times. That's just how it is, and there's nothing wrong with that. To pretend otherwise is to continue believing the lie that we are capable. We can conquer. We are not vulnerable.

When we all know, deep down, we are.

So like these seven nameless women in the Gospels, we are—when we dare to admit it—out of resources. Like them, we cannot get "clean" on our own. None of them was whole, and none of us are either. And never will be this side of heaven. That's simply the truth. A desperate one, but true nonetheless.


## The Good News

The courage and honesty of these women, however, invites us to be real as well, to quit pretending we're better than we really are or in command of our lives at all. We're not. That's the bad news at first, but it's really the good news. Great news, in fact, because it means we can stop trying to live up to expectations of being "good enough" when we know we never will be; we can admit we will never be smart enough, strong enough, talented or savvy or organized enough to become righteous in God's eyes. And thankfully, we don't have to.

That's the fairy tale of the gospel—the one that is still too good *not* to be true.

The great point of these women's stories—from the Samaritan woman at the well and the crippled woman in the synagogue to the widow of Nain, the prostitute, and the Canaanite woman—is that the presence of Jesus Christ alone made the difference for their desperate states. Chances were their lives did not suddenly become magically glamorous because of their encounter with Jesus; they were still women, after all, living in an oppressive, male-dominated culture. They would still face cultural marginalization or social alienation. Many were economically poor, and that likely wouldn't change. All of them would know the decay of their human bodies as they aged, even though some of them had experienced the miracle of restored health from the touch of Christ. And of course, each of these women would experience firsthand the day when their bones no longer moved, their hearts no longer beat, their lungs no longer filled with air. Though they could sidestep it or delay it, death was inevitable.

In other words, even *after* their interaction with the Man from Nazareth, life was still going to be hard for them—full of conflicts, heartaches, and obstacles that would confound and challenge them. So what difference did Jesus make for these obscure women who, for all we know, probably never went on to experience even a morsel of the comfortableness most of us know in modern America? What possible impact could the short amount of time they'd spent with that popular young rabbi have made for them as they went about their daily first-century lives by the Sea of Galilee? How were they better for it?

First, because he was no ordinary teacher, Jesus was deeply moved to respond to their physical circumstances—and cared extravagantly about them. Yet he was keenly aware that their earthly lives (like his) were only a shadow of what was to come. A blip on the eternal screen of something far grander. His priority on earth was always to address the interior matters of their lives; to the woman at the well, he gave eternal satisfaction to quench her restless soul. To the woman with the issue of blood, he offered freedom to be herself. To the woman of deformity, he restored her to her true purpose: to worship God. And to the woman whose tears washed his feet, he extended the amazing gift of grace and forgiveness that would provide deep and abiding rest. Each gift was spiritual, changing the course of their lives on earth and literally giving them a new lease for the remaining time they had. But because of the Word made Flesh, each woman was invited into an eternal friendship with the God of the universe. Forever. Unending. Infinite.

---

That truth alone is what sustains us in the here and now. Not an idol, not a human, not a formula for spirituality, not a dream or a lifestyle. None of those are guaranteed; all of those can change in a second. Only the presence of the One who was and is and is to come was their distinguishing hope and our way forward. His is the one true story that's truer than all the others, more desperate than any circumstance we face. A tale born and tried in love, which continues through the ages, one that calls us to respond.

A musician and worship leader friend I know helps prepare people on earth for what we'll do in heaven: worship. She sings of this reality in a wonderful old hymn, in words (and sounds) too beautiful to ignore:

> Come ye sinners poor and needy
> Weak and wounded sick and sore
> Jesus ready stands to save you
> Full of pity love and power.
> Come ye thirsty
> Come and welcome
> God's free bounty glorify
> True belief and true repentance
> Every grace that brings us nigh.
>> I will rise and go with Jesus
>> He will embrace me in His arms
>> And in the arms of my dear Savior
>> Oh there are ten thousand charms.
>> Oh there are ten thousand charms.
> Come ye weary heavy-laden
> Lost and ruined by the fall
> If you tarry until you're better
> You may never come at all.
>> I will rise and go with Jesus
>> He will embrace me in His arms
>> And in the arms of my dear Savior
>> Oh there are ten thousand charms.[2]

### The Best Yet

The invitation from Jesus to "arise and go with him" remains as passionate today as it did almost two thousand years ago. For just as he invited each nameless woman into the arms of her dear Savior to let him love her, so does he invite us to do the same. And if we have any question of that love, we need only look to the turning point of all human history, when Jesus Christ was condemned to die by callous government officials, abandoned by his friends, and thrust onto a cross, nails in hands and feet, thorns pressed into his skull. It was love that drove him there, that died a death you and I should have—for our own impurities and sins, the very attributes that still keep us from coming to God. And yet it was love that came alive again three days later, appearing first to a few grieving women, then hundreds of witnesses, and revealing himself still to each of us today.

It is love that still tells the stories of these women whose names we don't know. Why? Because their names are not hidden from the One whose home is called the City of God, the one who promises in John's Revelation to give new names to all who come to him as they join him in their eternal home. For in the promise of his presence comes the promise of a new identity, a new name, a new opportunity to live and breathe and pray and serve in his kingdom of hope. To be a part of something far more significant than this earthly existence. To feel no longer the suffocating bondage of our pasts or our cultures or our failures but to experience instead the sustaining joy and freedom that come when the only thing we're desperate for each day is Jesus.

There is no other Man like him. And there is no adventure like that of living with him, reveling in his love, participating in his purposes, marveling at his mysteries and wonders, and belonging to an eternal family with an eternal home. Nothing comes close.

Because nothing is like, as the old hymn says, "the deep, deep love of Jesus! Vast, unmeasured, boundless, free. Rolling as a mighty ocean in its fullness over me. Underneath me, all around me, is the current of thy love; leading onward, leading homeward, to thy glorious rest above."[3]

# Final Reflections

Each of these stories and passages remind us of our ongoing need for God's grace, to be a part of his Kingdom story. But we cannot accomplish this on our own abilities. We are desperate for the Good News of the gospel truth, every day. How can you apply each of the Scriptures in the Digging Deeper sections to your life?

What specifically can you and your community—for we cannot grow without the mutual support and help of others—do regularly to live out this faith with confidence and humility?

*What or who are we most thirsty for?*
    Lord, may we drink of you.

*How do we live with our brokenness?*
    Lord, may we stand in your strength and praise you.

*In what ways can we sacrifice for, and give to, your people?*
    Lord, may we be rich in your presence.

*How can we publicly reflect your healing hand?*
    Lord, may we seek you in all things.

*What fears, disappointments, and losses can we lay at your feet?*
    Lord, may we be changed by the hope of your
        resurrection.

*How can we begin to confess our sins, shames, and shortcomings?*
    Lord, may we revel in your love and grace.

*What might keep us from asking boldly for your help?*
    Lord, may we expect with humility and gratitude
        your ongoing promises to be fulfilled.

May we be desperate for truth and story.

# NOTES

### Prologue  Desperate . . . for a Story

1. Frederick Buechner, *Telling the Truth: The Gospel as Tragedy, Comedy and Fairy Tale* (San Francisco: Harper & Row, 1977), 98.
2. Ibid.

### Chapter 1  Thirsty for More Than a Drink

1. Song lyrics from *Man of La Mancha* are used by permission. © 1965 Andrew Scott Music, Helena Music Company. Words: Joe Darion. Music: Mitch Leigh.
2. Ibid.
3. Charles Haddon Spurgeon, *Spurgeon's Sermons: Volumes 3–4* (Grand Rapids: Baker, 1996).
4. Song lyrics from *Man of La Mancha*.

### Chapter 2  Bent, Battered, and Broken

1. Charles Spurgeon, "Unfit for Religious Instruction."

### Chapter 3  Empty Pockets

1. Edith Deen, *All of the Women of the Bible* (San Franciso: Harper & Row, 1983), 353.

### Chapter 5  Dead Woman Walking

1. Michael Joseph Gross, *Virtual Memories* http://virtual-memorials.com/main.php?action= resources.

2. C. S. Lewis, *A Grief Observed* (San Franciso: HarperSanFrancisco, 1961), 11.

3. Ibid., 16.

4. Ibid., 17–18.

## Chapter 6  Cry Me a River

1. Eugene Peterson, *Subversive Spirituality* (Grand Rapids: Eerdmans, 1994), 133–34.

2. Spurgeon, *Spurgeon's Sermons: Volumes 3–4.*

3. C. S. Lewis, *Letters to an American Lady*, ed. Clyde S. Kilby (Grand Rapids: Eerdmans, 1986).

## Chapter 7  Hustling for Scraps

1. Deen, *All of the Women of the Bible*, 190.

## Epilogue  A Desperate Truth

1. John Stott and David L. Edwards, "Essentials" (London: Hodder and Stoughton, 1988). Excerpted from *Authentic Christianity* (Downers Grove: Inter-Varsity Press).

2. Lyrics by Joseph Hart, 1759.

3. Lyrics by Samuel T. Francis, 1875.

# BIBLIOGRAPHY

The following, in some way or another, helped shape my thinking about Jesus as he interacted with these nameless women in the Gospels:

Barnes, M. Craig. *Yearning: Living Between How It Is and How It Ought to Be.* Downers Grove: InterVarsity Press, 1991.

Bowman, Most Rev. Dr. Robert M. *Sermon for Third Sunday in Lent, Cycle A.* www.rmbowman.com/catholic/s990307h.htm, March 7, 1999.

Bruce. F. F., ed. *The International Bible Commentary with the New International Version.* Grand Rapids: Zondervan, 1979.

Buechner, Frederick. *Telling the Truth: The Gospel as Tragedy, Comedy and Fairy Tale.* San Francisco: Harper & Row, 1977.

Deen, Edith. *All of the Women of the Bible.* San Francisco: Harper & Row, 1983.

Dinesen, Isak. *Babette's Feast and Other Anecdotes of Destiny.* Edited by Martha Levin. New York: Knopf, 1988.

Keener, Craig S. *A Commentary on the Gospel of Matthew.* Grand Rapids: Eerdmans, 1999.

Lewis, C. S. *A Grief Observed*. San Francisco: HarperSanFrancisco, 1961.

Lewis, C. S. *Letters to an American Lady*. Edited by Clyde S. Kilby. Grand Rapids: Eerdmans, 1986.

Marshall, Howard. *The Gospel of Luke: A Commentary on the Greek Text*. Grand Rapids: Eerdmans, 1978.

Newbigin, Lesslie. *The Light Has Come: An Exposition of the Fourth Gospel*. Grand Rapids: Eerdmans, 1982.

Nielson, Kathleen Buswell. *Continue to Live in Him: Ten Studies in Colossians and Philemon*. Lookout Mountain, GA: Covenant College, 2000.

O'Connor, Flannery. *The Collected Works of Flannery O'Connor*. New York: The Library of America Literary Classics, 1988.

Peterson, Eugene. *The Message: The New Testament in Contemporary Language*. Colorado Springs: NavPress, 1993.

———. *Masters of Imagination*, originally published in 1989 in *Eternity*, reprinted in *Subversive Spirituality*. Grand Rapids: Eerdmans, 1994, 1997.

Ryken, Leland, ed. *The Christian Imagination: The Practice of Faith in Literature and Writing*. Colorado Springs: Shaw Books, 2002.

Smith, Jami. "Wash Over Me" album. www.jamismith.com.

Spurgeon, Charles Haddon. *Spurgeon's Sermons: Volumes 3–4*. Grand Rapids: Baker, 1996.

Stott, John and David L. Edwards. "Essentials." London: Hodder and Stoughton, 1988. Excerpted from *Authentic Christianity*. Downers Grove: InterVarsity Press.

Wright, Vinita Hampton. *Velma Still Cooks in Leeway*. Nashville: Broadman and Holman, 2000.

———. *The Soul Tells a Story: Engaging Creativity with Spirituality in the Writing Life*. Downers Grove: InterVarsity Press, 2005.

# ACKNOWLEDGMENTS

A single book is always the result of the kindness of many people, and so I wish to express my sincere gratitude to:

Bob Hosack and the friends at Baker Publishing Group, who've always exemplified grace, professionalism, and integrity to me in publishing, and as a result greatly encourage me in my writing.

Reverend Sean Gilbert, who first encouraged me that these women's stories were as inspiring and important for men as they are for women.

Katherine Leary, who connected me with the great women at our home church, Redeemer Presbyterian Church in New York City, and Andrea Clark Mungo, Honja Metroka, Connie Metroka Ricci, Melissa Gorton, and Francis Nelson, who supported me as we retreated together to initially explore these nameless women in the Gospels.

The women at Dix Hills Evangelical Free Church in Long Island, New York; S.A.L.T. Ministry in Cresskill, New Jersey; the Fellowship of Christian Athletes So-Cal and the East Coast (Donna Noonan, Sue Semrau, Debbie Haliday, Jane Albright, Genevieve Wilkinson, Jen Price, Jami Smith,

Janet Hubble, Sue Kelly, Molly Shull, and the others!); all of whom allowed me to bounce off their great minds these ideas and stories at each gathering.

Cheryl Baird, Sue Roman, Donna Scott, Kristen Mapstone, and my other new friends in the women's ministry at Blanchard Alliance Church in Wheaton, Illinois, who modeled community to me and offered keen insights, authentic devotion, and downright inspiring insights as we explored these women together.

Eileen Sommi, my new writing colleague and Anne of Green Gables–type kindred friend whose "desperate" devotion to Jesus inspires me.

And of course the man in my life who reads everything I write and responds with astute theological insight and sensitive observations, my husband and partner in stories, Chris Gilbert.

Thank you, Reader, as well for traveling with me through the wonderful gift of story from the greatest book ever published. How kind of God Almighty to allow us to know him together through Word and Flesh and one another's stories.

May the adventure continue . . .

**Jo Kadlecek** is a former waitress, soccer player, and high school debate teacher who writes full time from her home on the Jersey Shore, just south of New York City. She is a frequent teacher at workshops, retreats, and conferences, and in the fall of 2006 joins the faculty of Gordon College in Wenham, MA. She holds a Master of Arts degree in communication and another in humanities. For more information about Jo and her writing, please visit her website at www.lamppostmedia.net.

Other books by Jo Kadlecek

Fiction
*A Mile from Sunday*, book 1 in the Lightfoot Trilogy
*The Sound of My Voice*

Nonfiction
*Fear: A Spiritual Navigation*, a memoir
*Reckless Faith: Living Passionately as Imperfect Christians*,
    a study on the life of Peter
*Feast of Life: Spiritual Food for Balanced Living*

"Jo beautifully pairs God's provision with our very personal desperations. Turning her writer's pen on the subtle, secondary women of Scripture, she underlines how Jesus meets our needs and enables us to see his presence in our own daily desperations."

—Elisa Morgan, CEO and president, MOPS International

"I have read the biblical accounts of these seven nameless women so many times before, but this time was very different. As Jo shared her insights into the lives of these women who experienced Jesus himself in the face of extreme pain and hopelessness, I found myself being drawn into a deeper personal understanding of the depth of the mercy, love, and forgiveness of Christ. I highly recommend this book for both men and women who want to receive a greater understanding of what it means to be a representative of Christ to a world that is desperate to know him."

—Nancy Alcorn, president and founder, Mercy Ministries

"Although conflicts, heartaches, and obstacles will always be before us, this book is a reminder that an encounter with Christ gives us hope for satisfaction, freedom, grace, forgiveness, and purpose. Jesus gave hope to these desperate women and extends the same invitation to the desperation in us all. He is our find; he is our prize; and we are his."

—Jami Smith, worship leader and musician, www.jamismith.com

"Jo Kadlecek is a gifted writer! *Desperate Women of the Bible* is an inspiring, prayerful resource for anyone who wants to know more about women in the Scriptures. The women on these pages come alive as Kadlecek skillfully adds contemporary anecdotes and personal stories that help us realize that solutions to many of today's problems are to be found in the Bible and the gospel of love given to us by the Lord."

—Amy Hill Hearth, coauthor of the New York Times bestseller *Having Our Say: The Delany Sisters' First 100 Years*

"I have found in *Desperate Women of the Bible* a careful teaching on Scripture that invites me to Jesus. Jo has given us an insightful gift into Christ's ways with women. I remember why I love him as I read the stories here. I think many will be blessed by the truth brought to light in this book."

—Debbie Haliday, regional camp director, Southern California Fellowship of Christian Athletes

"Jo Kadlecek's writing draws me in, and her insight takes me deep. Her personal stories complement the stories in the Scripture and make relevant the lives of these 'desperate women.'"

—Sue Semrau, head women's basketball coach, Florida State University